Missing LOVE Child

Eugene Lee McDuffie

2001-2007

Copyright © 2013 by Eugene Lee McDuffie

Missing Love Child
by Eugene Lee McDuffie

Printed in the United States of America

ISBN 9781628710243

All rights reserved solely by the author. The author guarantees all contents are original and do not infringe upon the legal rights of any other person or work. No part of this book may be reproduced in any form without the permission of the author. The views expressed in this book are not necessarily those of the publisher.

Unless otherwise indicated, Bible quotations are taken from the King James Version.

www.xulonpress.com

Table of Contents

Introduction ix

1. Searching For A Missing Love 13
2. I Was Missing Hugs 31
3. Love Is The Ingredient Missing 43
4. Hush Boy Love Made Me Beat You 53
5. Life In The Park 63
6. Love Healed Me 69
7. Missing Light In My Life 75

Dedication

I dedicate this book to all those friends that have helped me and supported me. Thank you for your support!
Eugene McDuffie

"Love is a fabric which never fades, no matter how often
it is washed in the water of adversity and grief."
Author unknown.

Disclaimer: The names have been changed to protect the innocent, and any actual similarities are not to be considered actual due to the book being fictionalized for literary entertainment purposes.

Introduction

I was born in the sixties. I do not remember much about my toddler years. It has been over fifty years of silence. I enjoy living my life and look forward to a new beginning of every day. I enjoy music, singing, horticulture, creative arts, and sports. It makes my heart smile when I hear or read about the many achievements in life of the people I have been so blessed to meet. I am always excited when I hear about the people who learned to live their lives to their fullest potential; overcome life hardship obstacles.

Over the many years I have had so many struggles and obstacles that I had to overcome by myself. Believe it or not, the most difficult and most painful times in my life have helped me to become the person I am today. Truly, I know if it had not been for Grace and Mercy, I would not be writing these words that I am sharing with you all. Back in those days, I would have never thought I would be able to survive to live to be the age I am now. I could never put all the words in this book. There would never be enough pages to tell it all.

The many tears I recall crying as a young boy would have filled the Niagara Falls. In my heart, I felt compelled in 2001 to spend seven years of my life writing this story "Missing Love Child." Let me tell you the reason I want to share my story with you. The main reason is to help someone. My desire for this book is that someone will read these pages and find hope and strength to survive whatever emotional pain they may be experiencing in their life. My hope is as you read the pages in this story; its message will help you to break free from the silence of your adult or childhood pain.

This is my objective, and I am personally dedicated to this goal in spite of how difficult it is for me to recall circumstances in my own life that brought me hurt, shame and pain! I am honored to be a recipient of the Human Relations Award in 2002. I received this award because of the work I started with Youth in Action Now, by helping children stay out of gangs. Thank you! My mission also has been to help those that are in chains to gang bondage.

I personally know today the joy and liberty of what it means to be truly free! Many of the individuals I've been so blessed to meet and help were cross addicted, ex-gang members, disadvantaged youth and the homeless. I also want to tell you at this time; I do not pretend to be an expert in any medical professional field. I have been fortunate to live through many hardships and obstacles in life. These hardships and trials and circumstances that I have chosen to learn from, have collectively been the greatest Teacher in my own personal life.

This Teacher I gave a name, and I choose to call this Teacher: Mr. LIFE. I just wish I had only been more attentive when I was younger. I was not a great student back in those days as a young boy growing up. When I was young boy, I thought I knew it all. Now, I'm older and as I am writing, I'm thinking; would it really have made a difference? Could I, or should I, have acted any differently if I were given a second chance? I realize now, Life does not give you a formula or step by step instructions. Life is about every individual doing what is right and just, and making the right choices for your life and the lives of others.

The greatest gift anyone can give another human being is the gift of love. I am grateful to know and have experienced the greatest gift of Love in my life! It doesn't matter how old I get I will never forget that day when I first met a boy named Penny.

If you're reading this, it's imperative to me that you understand who I am. What it was like for me as a young boy living with the woman I call "Mama" and the man I call my "Papa." It is very troubling to me now that I am a little older and definitely a little wiser. When I hear individuals say; "I know him or her," the reason this

Introduction

comment troubles me is because you could be with someone your entire life and not know who that person really is at all.

Then Penny says; let me continue telling you a little bit about what life was really like for me growing up and living with my Mama and Papa. I was their child and I was a good boy. All I ever wanted to do was please my Mama and Papa. Oh! My name is Penny everyone calls me Pee for short since the very day I was born into this world. Except for my Papa; he calls me Penny and I am not sure why. I never understood why Mama or Papa chose to name me Penny, especially since all the other children made fun of me and my name at school and at home.

My Mama was the first person to call me by the name Pee, for short. I want to mention I grew up in a home where people did not hug or talk or show their feelings. Never would you hear these words "I love you" in the home I grew up in. Mama and Papa always found other things in their life to hug and one of those they chose to hug or love, definitely wasn't me. Soon the words, "Missing Love Child" became my life, which soon would become a reality for me. I would hide deep in my heart, until now. A cold hard fact in my life, eventually I would learn to grow and accept and never ever dare question. I accepted the fact it was the horrible life I had been born with. Besides what could I have done about my life anyway? I was just a child.

I was so young and confused and thought my life was just fine. I stay away from asking Papa or Mama too many questions. I knew it would just get them mad at me. I just thought, I am being treated the way I'm supposed to be treated. All children were treated by their Mama and Papa the way I was, or so I thought. I made a promise to myself I would "HUSH MY MOUTH." It's a miracle I survived at all back in those miserable days. I always thought there was something seriously wrong with me as a little boy. My mind had so many negative thoughts. Thoughts I could never keep up with no matter how hard I tried. Mama and Papa would have their friends and family members over all the time. I was never good enough for Mama or Papa to introduce me to their friends or family. I learned as a boy how to disappear at a very young age and stay quiet. Papa told me never to tell my Mama anything! My Mama told me never to tell

Missing Love Child

Papa anything. Then Penny would sigh and his words to me were; "I never had love Mr. Eugene. Love is what I missed in my life." Penny had experienced firsthand such heartache and emotional pain at such a young age.

The Heartache experience can destroy a child's goals; dreams and life. I was thinking lately now that I've grown to be an adult; why is it that so many Children in our society often don't feel love or receive love anyway? A child does not ask to come into this world. The birth of a child is a Miracle. I believe every child deserves to be loved, protected and provided for, unconditionally. There are many people and children searching around the world for Love. Just like Penny's search for love from people and things that would never be able to give them love back. Just imagine living your whole entire life like Penny did, in silence or "hushing your mouth." Suddenly, you finally realize that there wasn't one person in this entire universe that LOVED or cared about you. Then Penny told me; "All I knew how to do, Mr. Eugene, as I was growing older was too "HUSH my mouth!" I knew I had to keep silent and never tell anybody."

It's really difficult to revisit the past or think about the childhood you may have experienced or may still be experiencing. Especially the awful times you felt that nobody loved or cared about you. Penny said; "Nobody ever hugged me or told me they loved me. Nobody, not my Mama or Papa. Nobody in this world spoke the words; "I love you Penny," to me. Wow!! Imagine if nobody spoke those words to you for a second. "Nobody hugs me or tells me they love me."

Those were the first words I heard when I met Penny on that day. Penny today, has grown to be an adult. I still will never forget the day when I met Penny and he said to me; "My name is Penny, if I had just been loved by someone or anyone in this world, my life would have been better. Why would my Mama and Papa choose to love a boy like me named Penny anyway? Mama wanted a girl and my Papa just knew in his heart I was going to be a girl, too. I missed love as a child, I know now love was always missing in my home and life."

Chapter 1

Searching For a Missing Love

It was a cold, miserable day. I was not about to go outside. I will never forget that day, because it felt like snow was coming and it was ice cold outside and inside Mama and Papa's house. I do remember Papa saying there was not enough money to pay for oil. I remember that day as if it was yesterday. This is what I remember and how it all began. Mama and my Papa were very busy in the house on that cold day. They were planning their big family reunion. I sat there and watched as my Mama popped some pills in her mouth and of course, Papa had a few drinks on that cold day. This was not unusual. Papa drank booze like a fish seven days a week and three hundred and sixty five days out of the year.

There was an excitement in the air throughout the house on that night. Mama and Papa were very excited, I was not. I did not understand or know what all the excitement was about. I guess it was because Papa and Mama had relatives coming to see them from out of town. I still didn't understand what the big deal was. Besides, I really didn't know Mama's or Papa's relatives at all. Their relatives had never visited our house ever before, or even met me. I had no idea who these people were anyway, coming to Mama's and Papa's house. I had just turned eleven years old and my birthday had just passed. It was difficult for me to feel excited about people I had never met or did not know at all. I couldn't understand the reason why I should make a big deal about relatives that never even bothered to meet me.

I remember hurrying home on that day because I was so excited about it being my birthday. All day long I kept thinking about what Mama and Papa had got for me on my birthday. I ran into the house from school and then Mama yelled; "Pee, I didn't have money to do anything for your birthday this year. We have a lot of important things to buy that are more important than your birthday. You do realize your Papa and I are getting everything ready for our family reunion this year. You're Papa and I will celebrate your birthday with you on another day. I know you understand, Pee you will have other birthdays anyway."

I wanted to speak, instead, I hushed my mouth and dared not question what Mama was saying to me about my birthday. In my mind, I had no clue what Mama was talking about "other birthdays anyway." My birthday was today, that I was all I could think about. I acted like I was not disappointed; half smiled and walked back upstairs to my room.

Really, I was very disappointed in my heart and angry. I still pretended and acted as if I was not disappointed. I told myself there will be other birthdays. I didn't care about getting a present from Mama or Papa on my birthday. I would have just been happy to hear Mama or Papa say I love you Penny! The words I love you Penny, or Pee, on my birthday; on that day never happened for me from Mama or Papa. I just wanted to close my eyes and disappear or sleep and forget about that cold, miserable, awful, stupid birthday!

Papa came home from work. I knew in my heart trouble was about to begin for me. Papa always would come into the house hungry and half loaded from going out with his friends after work. Papa would meet his friends at a bar before he came home. Papa never would take a lunch to work. He would be starving when he came home. I should tell you, my Papa never called me the name, Pee. My Papa always called me Penny from the day I was born. Mama always calls me by the name Pee my entire life.

Papa would often tell me. "Penny boy, you know a real man doesn't waste any time eating when he supposed to be working, boy. Penny, how many times have I told you a man does not cry?!

Penny, hush your mouth and stop whining like a little girl! Hush your mouth boy, unless I tell you to speak!" I quickly said; "Ok, Papa," and then ran upstairs to my room as usual. This was a routine I was used to doing around Papa.

My Papa always made sure he reminded me about how real boys or men should behave and real boys or men never cry, according to my Papa. I would often spend a lot of my time in my room alone, looking at the four walls. I did not want to be in my Mama or Papa's way, and Mama and Papa like the fact I stay out of their way and in my room.

Every day after school, I run upstairs and would hang my coat in the closet in my room. I look over at the door and saw on the door a calendar that I had hung on the back of my closet door. I had marked the date of my birthday on the calendar with a blue marker that was also hanging on my closet door. Blue was just one of my favorite colors. I had a few favorite colors. Then I thought, "What's going on with Mama and Papa anyway?" I should have known then that the rest of my birthdays weren't going to be happy ones after that miserable birthday. Mama and Papa were so busy planning their family reunion that nothing else seemed to matter. They never even thought about saying "Happy Birthday" to me. I still remember crying myself to sleep as I sat on my bed in my room on that evening. Their stupid family reunion was all they had on their minds. They just ignored me as if I was never in the house with them on my birthday. I didn't understand what was happening and why.

I had this cold, awful feeling in my gut that made me almost vomit on the evening of my birthday. A tear fell from my eyes as I was thinking about my birthday. A thought came to my mind about the words Mama spoke to me on my birthday; "There will be other birthdays anyway." I quickly wiped the tears away from my eyes before I went back downstairs.

Papa didn't like me crying at all and I did not want Papa to see me crying or it would be big problem for me. If Papa did see me crying, he would make fun of me. My Papa always says; "You're supposed to be a boy and a real boy never cries his eyes out like little girls do, or a baby does. Are you a boy or a little girl or a baby Penny?" I wasn't about to go downstairs with one tear on my face.

I knew Papa would disapprove and I would be made fun of for the rest of the night.

I tried to think about happy things that happened when I was at school that day. Then I heard Mama yelling, "Pee, come downstairs boy. It's time to eat supper." I ran downstairs as fast as my feet would take me and sat down at the dining table with Mama and Papa. I thought finally, Mama and Papa are going to talk to me about school or my birthday. Then Mama says, "Pee how was school today? Did you do your homework?"

I always knew when Mama had a couple of those happy pills or a drink of alcohol. Mama would always ask me about school and be more talkative to me than usual. I said, "Mama we had a substitute teacher today; our regular teacher was out sick." Then Papa interrupted loudly; "Forget about that school stuff, besides we have more important things to talk about -hush your mouth, Penny!"

I just kept my mouth shut out of fear. I knew never to talk back to Papa or Mama. I knew what would happen if I opened my big mouth. "What are you planning on making for dinner for our relatives that are coming for this big family reunion?" Papa asked Mama. I just sat there looking to Mama and Papa as they both just kept talking and interrupting each other. I watched Papa slurring his words, he had almost finished all the bottles of liquor he had sitting on the table. The more alcohol Papa drank, the louder Papa was yelling, and the more spit got all over the dinner table as he spoke.

I didn't eat much dinner on that night, I suddenly lost my appetite. I lost my appetite after listening to them and watching Papa spit all over the food. Then I said to Mama and Papa, "I'm finished eating my dinner, I am not hungry. May I please be excused to go to my room?" I could not believe it! Mama and Papa kept right on talking over each other, as if I never asked Mama a question at all. As if they never heard one word I spoke.

Both my parents did not make sense to me at all on that night. Then I thought, it really wouldn't matter to them if I left the table anyway. They acted as if I wasn't sitting with them at all. So, what did it matter if I walked away from the table, anyway? I got up out of the chair very quietly and put my dish in the sink, like I always did. I went to my room because I thought it would be ok with Mama and Papa. Besides, I was not hungry and wanted to listen to some music in my room.

I couldn't have been in my room for five seconds. Then I heard Mama yelling my name; "Pee, where are you boy? Get down here Pee, NOW!" When my Mama would yell my name, Papa would always yell my name too. The funny thing about this is, my Papa didn't know why he was yelling my name. Then Papa starts yelling my name louder than Mama.

I used to feel like Mama and Papa were having a yelling contest to see which of them could yell my name the loudest. Of course, Papa always won the yelling contest. Papa yells, "Penny, I know you didn't get up from the table without asking to be excused boy." I ran fast downstairs and sat back down at the dining table. Then they both started talking to each other again, making not any sense at all to me. I just sat there listening. I just stared at them confused. I was too afraid to speak or get out of my seat again.

I noticed Papa had his six pack bottles of beer out on the table. I knew it was going to be a long night for me. I sat there in the chair at the dining table for hours. Until I lost track of the time, I just sat there at the table watching Papa drink his beer and spit all over the table as he was talking. Eventually I disappeared. I felt I was invisible. Neither Papa nor Mama could see or hear me.

I was being forced to listen to absolutely nothing. I didn't understand why I couldn't leave the table. Especially since nobody was talking to me anyway. Besides, I had to go the bathroom and was about to urinate in my clothes. Yet I was too afraid to get up or ask Papa if I could go to the bathroom. They just kept on talking about their plans for their big family reunion. It was more important, Papa said, than asking about how school was for me or about my birthday.

I wasn't about to get out of the seat again without their permission. I could tell Papa was starting to feel the effects from his booze bottles that he had proudly displayed on the table. It was getting late and I was getting sleepy; I had to go to the bathroom. What could I do? It was a no-win situation. Until Papa finally says; "Penny, what the heck are you still doing up? Take your little butt to bed boy! You betta not be late for school tomorrow." I was so happy to go to bed;

quickly I got up out of the seat from the table. I said to Papa and Mama; "I hope you have a good night, Mama and Papa."

Papa or Mama never answered me or said one word back to me. Never even looked in my direction, as I walked away sad, puzzled and troubled. I ran to the bathroom as fast as my legs would let me. Then I went to bed feeling really upset. I just could not sleep. I didn't understand why Mama or Papa that night acted as if I was invisible. I remember crying myself to sleep on my eleventh birthday.

I came home the next day excited about an art project I completed at school. The art teacher taught us how to make an animal shape out of clay. When my clay project got finished, it turned out to be a puppy dog. I was so excited and couldn't wait to get home and tell Mama. I always wanted a puppy, but Papa does not like dogs.

Mama always said; "There is no way in hell a dog is coming in this house. I barely got enough food just taking caring of you, Pee. Besides, there are way too many mouths to feed in this house already." I couldn't wait to show Mama and Papa when I got home from school on that day what I made in my class.

My Papa's brother was at our house when I got home from school. They had already spent time drinking their share of the beer and booze bottle. I could smell it as I entered the house; they both stunk and smelled like booze. I guess Papa's brother arrived early to help Papa setup for the big family reunion. I ran inside the house yelling. "Papa, I have to show you something I made at school. Papa, please take a look at the clay dog I made in school today."

Papa quickly put his hand over my mouth and told me, "Penny, hush your big stupid mouth boy. Can't you see your Uncle is here helping me setup for this family reunion? I don't want to hear your mouth, Penny. How many times Penny, did I tell you not to be running your mouth if adults are talking? Penny, you talk too much."

I stayed quiet and obeyed Papa, walking away feeling sad and mad at the same time. Then I thought, "Go show Mama what you made!" I started yelling again, "Mama!" I ran up the steps as fast as I could. I got up the stairs and saw Mama cleaning. I knew Mama would want to see the art project I made at school. Then I said to Mama; "Look at what I made in art class today at school out of clay."

Searching For a Missing Love

My Mama just stared at me with this glossy look in her eyes. I knew then she had some of her pills by the look on her face, while I was at school. Mama says; "Pee, I really don't have time boy to be looking at some stupid clay dog." I started to speak, and then Mama interrupted me and said, "HUSH your mouth. Stay in a child's place! Why are you always making that crazy stuff anyway? I got my nephews and nieces sleeping in this house tomorrow and lot of stuff on my mind. I have to get everything ready for them."

I just stared at her, thinking and wondering, "Why is it that Mama doesn't care about what I do or make at school anymore?" Then Mama yelled, "Get your butt the hell out of my way, Pee! I am too busy for your nonsense." I went back to my room sat down on my bed staring at the dog I made out of clay, thinking to myself. "Penny, it's just a stupid art thing anyway. Nobody really cares about the stupid clay dog you made at school."

I stood up in front of my bed, mad; staring at the clay puppy dog I made at school. I dropped my puppy dog of clay on the floor and watched it break into a thousand pieces on that night. I felt my young heart shattered into a thousand pieces on that miserable night. On that night, all I could think about was those awful words spoken to me by my own Mama and Papa.

I started cleaning my room like Mama told me to do. Making sure I stayed out of Mama or Papa's way. Until Mama walked into my room while I was cleaning and says; "Pee, your Papa and I decided you are going to have to sleep downstairs in the basement on the nights of the Family reunion. Our family is going to be staying here with us in the house we need your room."

I just looked at Mama as if she was crazy or something. I was confused and not sure what to say to Mama. My first thought was, "I must be hearing things; I just disappear again." I thought in my mind, "Why do I have to sleep down there in the basement? Why?" I was scared and thought Mama would change her mind when she calmed down.

I didn't realize Mama was still speaking to me, until Mama yells out and says; "Are you deaf, stupid, dumb or what Pee boy! There's not enough room for you and my nephews in the same room. I will not have my family sleeping on the floor, you understand don't you

Pee?" I started crying and asked Mama, "What do you mean the basement? There's no bed downstairs in the basement. Mama, do you mean I will be sleeping on the floor with all the bugs and mice down there? What do you mean?"

Mama quickly says, "Hush your mouth boy! Pee, I don't want to hear anything more from your mouth. Stop whining like a little baby girl before I tell your Papa. That's just the way it's going to be. Besides, you can take that blanket with you downstairs. You sleep on it if you want. Just leave the pillow on your bed for my nephew to sleep on. I already told you this is a big family reunion; now hush your mouth everything has to be perfect for them."

I said, "Fine, Mama, I will sleep in the basement downstairs if that is what you want me to do." I really didn't have a choice anyway. I did not want to piss Mama off any more than what she already was. I knew better anyway to talk back to Mama, especially if she had that crazy look in her eyes.

I also knew that basement was going to be a dark, dirty, cold place for me. I really didn't want to sleep down there; I was shaking and scared to death. I didn't want to give Mama or Papa another thing to make fun of me about. I felt like disappearing if I was around my Mama or Papa. In those days, it was like I became invisible. I could see Mama and Papa but they could not see me or hear me. I would talk to Pee, myself, sometimes and sometimes I would talk to myself, Penny.

At long last, it was the big day of their family reunion. I just thought that Mama and Papa would be full of happiness and joy. My Mama's family was the first to arrive with all their children to our house. They got to the house earlier than what Mama expected. I sat there watching as they all entered into the living room. I just stared because I really didn't know any of Mama's Family. Mama's family did not know me either.

We all were meeting each other for the first time. I thought, "Why is it that I never met Mama's and Papa's family before? Is this because they both are both ashamed of me?" I saw all of Mama's family members standing there in the room. I just couldn't stop staring at them. Mama's nephew looked the same age as me; he was about my height. Mama's nephew and I just kept starring at each other.

I stood there quiet and that is when Mama started on me. I could tell just by the way Mama was talking loudly and how she was acting; that the stupid pill my Mama was taking was doing all the talking for her. Then Mama says, "Pee, come over here! Be a good Pee and take my nephew to the room he is going to be sleeping in while he is staying with us. You know the room I fixed up for him?" I asked Mama, "What room are you talking about? What room?" Mama says, "Pee you know the room, and you said he could sleep in your room while he is here for this reunion."

I looked at the other boy that looked exactly my age and was definitely my height. Then I looked over at my Mama, thinking to myself; "Pee you never wanted him or anyone to sleep in your room. Why would I want someone to occupy my bed while I sleep on a cold, nasty basement floor? I don't even know who this boy, Mama's nephew is. I was just told he was Mama's nephew by Mama; expected to give up my bed for him. Papa wanted to make sure he let all Mama's family members know how I gave up my room for this family reunion. I never said I wanted to give up my room up for this stupid reunion or Mama's nephew."

I kept trying to understand in my mind, but I just could not. No matter how hard I tried to understand, it was crazy on that night and made no sense to me at all. Then I realized; Penny, your Mama thinks her nephew is too good to sleep on a dirty basement floor. I'm not good enough to sleep in my own room for this family's big reunion. I just stared hard at Mama's nephew; Mama's nephew stares hard back hard at me, too.

I finally said, "Let me take you upstairs and show you the room you're going to be sleeping in." Mama's nephew looks at me and laughs like I told a joke or something. I couldn't understand what his stupid laughter was all about, it just made me angry. Especially, since I was the person that would be sleeping on that hard floor in that dirty basement. He was going to be sleeping in my bed, in my room, laughing. I felt there was nothing to laugh about at all. I was mad and hurt and really did not want to show him the room at all. I also did not want to hear Papa's feet running up the stairs, his mouth yelling at me in front of Mama's nephew.

I kept thinking as I was walking up the steps, then I had an idea. My room is plenty big enough for both of us to stay in anyway. I could sleep on the floor in my room. It didn't matter to me; at least it would be better than me sleeping on that cold, dirty basement floor. What I failed to realize was that sleeping on the basement floor was going to be a new thing that I would become accustomed to eventually.

I walked back downstairs to ask Mama if I could sleep on the floor in my room. Mama was busy talking to her sister and getting the dinner ready for everyone. Then I asked Mama again louder; "Can I PLEASE sleep on the floor in my room instead of the basement floor? There's plenty of room for the both of us."

Mama looked at her sister and then turned her head and looked over at me. Mama walked over toward me and grabbed me by my shirt collar and shakes me. Mama says, yelling and spitting in my face; "Pee, HUSH YOUR MOUTH! My nephew is sleeping in your room alone and you are sleeping in the basement! It's passed the time for you to go to your room downstairs and go to sleep. I thought you knew better to ask me anything when I am talking." I said, "Ok Mama," as the tears rolled down my face. I waited for Mama to let go of my shirt collar. I could hardly breathe. I quietly went downstairs to the basement thinking I should have kept my big stupid mouth shut. I couldn't understand what was going on. What was happening to me as I sat downstairs on the basement floor? Look at what you caused, Pee. It is your fault entirely. You should have hushed your mouth. What did I do to cause me to be sleeping on a basement floor?"

The other children were still awake upstairs; running, laughing, playing. I could hear their feet stomping across the floor and their laughter. Yet Mama refused to let me stay upstairs on the first night of their big family reunion. Nobody even cared if I was with them at their family reunion. I thought I was part of this family too, until tonight. Papa didn't care at all about me being downstairs in the basement. All Papa cared about that night at the reunion was drinking his alcohol was laughing and spitting on people when he talked.

I was feeling hungry downstairs in the basement. I could smell the food cooking. I had to get back upstairs. That was the only way I could get something to eat. I could hear from downstairs that everyone was having a good time upstairs. I just wanted something to eat; I was afraid to go back upstairs and ask for food. I did not want to make my Mama angrier than what she already was at me. I just told myself, Penny, walk back upstairs! I felt totally confused and I knew Papa was drunk and Mama was too busy talking to her family members. I wasn't sure what Mama would say to me next. I just remember shaking a lot and my stomach hurting real bad. I wasn't about to get Mama or Papa mad at me again or get into trouble more than I already was.

Mama and Papa already acted like they hated me and didn't want me around anymore. I was just about to walk up the stairs when I heard Papa's footsteps walking down the stairs. Papa says "Penny, I brought your plate of food down here, this way you don't get your Mama upset." I thought to myself, well, at least Papa brought me some food until I heard what he had to say next. Papa said, "There are not enough seats at the table for all you children to sit."

Reality hit me. Not only was I going to be sleeping on the basement floor, I was going to be eating my dinner sitting on the dirty basement floor too. "I'm sure you do not mind eating down here, do you Penny? Besides, you always are sitting at the table with us anyway. I can't have your Mama getting upset again. I heard how you ran your mouth off to your Mama. I didn't think she should send you anything to eat at all. Bad boys like you do not deserve to eat Penny. If it was just left up to me you would miss your supper tonight. You're always so cocky with your mouth, complaining and whining like a baby girl." Then Papa puts his hand on my shoulder and looks at me and smiles and says, "I understand you Penny. I'll be back down later and soon you will learn to be a good boy." I just stare at Papa confused. I wanted to say something; I was just too scared to speak. The words just wouldn't come out of mouth no matter how hard I tried to speak. I knew my Papa had a bad temper; I wasn't about to say anything to get my face slapped. I just did not know what Papa meant when he said; "I will be a good boy soon." I could smell the alcohol on him as he spit talked, laughing in my face.

I took the plate of food from Papa and quickly sat down on the blanket on the basement floor. Then Papa walked back upstairs laughing out loud to himself. I could hear Papa's laughter from all the way downstairs in the basement. I just stared at the plate of food and my hunger left me. I just could not get Papa's words out of my head. My stomach felt strange, like it was all tied up in knots. My appetite was gone. I finally went to sleep only to wake up from the nasty alcohol smell and Papa standing in front of me buckling up his pants, laughing. Papa looked into my eyes and then smiled. Papa left the basement fast and never spoke a word to me as he was leaving. I was not sure what he was smiling at me about. I didn't understand why Papa was fixing his belt buckle on his pants as I was waking up.

The next day came. It was Saturday, I walked upstairs quietly hoping Mama would still be sleeping from the pills she took last night. Instead, Mama and her sister were talking in the kitchen. Everybody appeared to be happy, to me. I thought it would be a good time to speak with Mama. Since she seemed like she was in such a happy mood. I walk over to my Mama and asked, "What's everybody so happy about Mama?" Then Mama stared at me angrily. I thought to myself; "Why did I ask Mama such a stupid question?" Mama says; "Pee, how long have we been talking to you about this special day, why are you acting so stupid?"

I looked at Mama puzzled. In my heart I knew my big mouth got me into trouble again. I didn't want Mama to yell at me again especially in front of her family. I really didn't know what day Mama was talking about or what would be the right answer to say back to Mama. Then I decided to say nothing at all. I thought in my head, "Penny, just stay quiet, I wouldn't say the wrong answer back to Mama." It got very quiet in the living room like the excitement was gone after I walked into the kitchen. Then Mama got angrier at me and she yells. "ANSWER ME ARE YOU DEAF PEE, OR JUST STUPID?" I quickly answered, "I don't know why everyone was so happy, that was all I said." I never even had a chance to get the next word out of my mouth. Mama takes her hand and slaps my face hard in front of her family members that were in the same room.

Mama says, "HUSH YOUR MOUTH! Just go back downstairs! Pee to your room and of my sight. Maybe your Papa will bring you something to eat down there." I went back to the basement with my face stinging and tears falling from my face. I sat again crying on the blanket that I lay out on the floor for myself to sleep on. I disappeared when I got back in the basement. I just close my eyes and disappeared. I didn't want to think about Mama or the way she slapped my face. I started yelling at myself in my head and out loud. "Pee, you're so stupid you should have never been born. Just disappear forever, this way you will make your Mama and Papa happy." Then another voice told me in my head "Hush your mouth!! Penny, if you were a good boy Mama and Papa would love you. Your Mama slaps you because you're not a good boy; this is why you are in the basement."

Then I started yelling out loud to myself in this angry voice and said; "Pee, you know your Mama and Papa do not care about or love you. It would have been better if you were never born." I kept wishing I was deaf so I wouldn't hear all the excitement upstairs and the other kids talking loud and having a good time. I just listened; I could hear my heartbeat as I sat there on my blanket on the basement floor. I started thinking about the nasty way Papa and Mama were treating me and it bothered me. It became clear to me in my mind and heart on that dreadful day; Papa or Mama don't love or care about me, that's why they put me downstairs in this basement. Nor did they want me upstairs for their great big family reunion or party. The more I thought about what was happening to me; reality hit me that I wasn't part of Papa's or Mama's family any longer. I was Pee, or Penny, a boy that nobody loved or cared about or wanted. The children Mama and Papa loved were playing upstairs and not in a basement like me.

As I sat in the basement on the blanket, I made sure I was as quiet like a mouse sneaking into a room. I did this quietly so I could at least hear what was going on upstairs. I thought maybe if I am very quiet Papa or Mama would come back downstairs and ask me to go upstairs with the rest of the family. I knew deep in my heart and in the back of my mind that was never going to happen anyway. All that seemed to matter was the big family reunion and making sure everyone else had a goodtime.

Papa did come back downstairs to tell me something on that day. I could smell the booze the closer Papa got to me. Papa was drunk again and I was scared, all I could see was the angry look he had in his eyes. Papa didn't tell me to go upstairs or what I thought it was going to be. Papa says to me; "Penny you shouldn't upset your Mother like you did today. You know her family came a very long way to be here. This is your Mama's big important day. Why are you upsetting your Mother, Penny? Our families will be leaving to go back to their own homes tomorrow." I never said a word back to Papa; I hushed my mouth like they always told me to do. I wasn't about to speak the wrong words again. I was too scared to speak anyway. All I did was just stare at Papa; I never spoke a word. Papa walked back up the stairs laughing out loud, to which made no sense to me.

I just sat there on that blanket in the basement thinking things will be better tomorrow for me. I will be back in my own room again; I will be sleeping in on my own bed. After this reunion thing is all over; I can't wait for it to be over. I felt asleep listening to the laughter from the other children upstairs. Thinking tomorrow will be better day for me by the way that better day never happened for me. Mama and Papa will treat me better after this reunion is all over, I thought.

Morning came and I quickly took off the blanket that was covering me up. Then I quickly pulled up my pajama pants. I thought to myself that they must have fallen down while I was sleeping tossing and turning. Quietly, I walked upstairs and watched Mama's family members hugging one another and saying their goodbyes to each other. Then Mama walks over to her nephew that was my age, eleven, and says to him; "You can come back here to stay anytime. You are such a good boy. I love having you here and the rest of the family as well."

I watched from a distance as Mama and Papa gave Mama's nephew a great big hug. I held back the tears from falling from my eyes. There was no way I was about to cry and get into more trouble. Pee told me in my head, Penny just disappears. I just could not watch Mama hugging her nephew like a teddy bear. I also could not remember the last time Mama or Papa hugged me. The voice in my head said; "Your Mama or Papa never hugs you Penny. You are too stupid to be hugged, stupid Pee! That's who you are."

Searching For a Missing Love

I was so disappointed and hurt inside when I saw Mama hugging her nephew. I thought I had heard and seen it all, I just couldn't believe it. Until I heard Mama said to her nephew again; "I love you! Come back and stay in Pee's room anytime." When I heard Mama said those words to her nephew it broke my heart even more. I couldn't remember when Mama or Papa said; I love you, to me. I never asked to come into this world, what is wrong with me? Why do Mama and Papa hate me so much?

The only words Mama or Papa said to me was, "stupid, shut up, or Hush your mouth." I stood there in the room with everyone else, not Mama or Papa or nobody else knew or cared if I was even there. I just disappeared again; it made me so upset that nobody even cared enough to introduce me to their family's members. I finally realized on that day that I was a nobody! I also had nobody that cared; I was a nobody! I never got to spend time with any of the family members at the reunion. Mama's nephew was good enough to sleep in my room, on the bed. I didn't even know what his name was. I was never properly introduced to him or anyone else.

I was just told to stay in the basement the entire time of the reunion. Some big family reunion, it just did not include me. An event in my parents' lives became more important than me. I thought I was part of the family too. After all, it was Mama's and Papa's family and they did not want me to spoil the reunion for them. I just knew Mama's nephew looked the same age as me. I stared into Mama's nephews eyes and Mama's nephew kept staring at me in my eyes. Mama's nephew smiled at me as he walked out the front door.

I just stood there feeling confused and mad. Mama's family left and never said goodbye to me. What I didn't realize was while I was standing there; my Papa was asking me a question. I never even heard his voice at all. Papa's family was still were saying their goodbyes to each other. They were the last to leave the house on that day. Papa yelled; "PENNY ANSWER ME I KNOW YOU HEARD ME BOY."

I didn't know how to answer Papa because I never even heard his question. Papa's speech was distorted. I knew he was drunk and I couldn't remember what he was talking about. I had disappeared again in my mind. I thought quickly, I have to say something quick.

I said the first thing that came to my mind and my words were; "Yes Papa, you're right." Then Papa yells, "Go back downstairs to the basement Penny, get out of my sight, you are so stupid. Just HUSH YOUR MOUTH! GO TO THE BASEMENT!" I started to walk away but before I could, Papa grabbed me by my arms and shakes me real hard. Then Papa said "PENNY, don't you ever turn your back to me or walk away from me again if I'm speaking to you, boy!"

I was so scared and said, "Yes Sir Papa, I hear you, I'm sorry." Then Papa let go of my arms and quickly I ran back to the basement fast and sat down on the blanket, scared. I still don't remember what exactly the question was Papa asked was asking me on that day. Time went by slow as I was sitting there that night on that blanket in the basement floor. Mama or Papa had not even come downstairs to talk or see me or bring me food. Days had gone by without me eating anything at all. My stomach was all tied up in knots.

On the days of the family reunion I would take the food off my plate that Papa would bring down to me that I didn't eat. Then I waited until Papa left and hid the food for later if I got hungry. This way, if I got hungry later or during the night I would have some food to eat. The main reason I did this was because Mama or Papa didn't bother to come downstairs at all sometimes at night to bring me anything to eat. I will never forget that day Papa shook me and made me urinate on myself.

I guess Mama or Papa didn't think I deserved to eat their food if they were mad at me. I am just not sure why Papa or Mama was so angry with me. It seems to me I always was doing something to make Mama and Papa angry with me. I am not sure on that day what I could have said or done to Mama or Papa that would have changed anything. I kept thinking if I tell them I'm sorry they won't be so mad or hate me so much.

Finally I fell asleep. I woke up the next morning my blanket and clothes were wet. I didn't remember spilling anything on my blanket before I went to sleep. I quick jumped up and felt my pajama pants with my hands; they were soaking wet. Then I felt so ashamed because I had urinated on myself in my sleep. I wasn't about to tell Mama or Papa what had happen to me on that night. I was too afraid of what they would say to me and just make me stay down in that dirty basement longer.

I was tired of being in that basement in the dark, watching the bugs crawl on the walls. Yet I knew I had to keep the urinating on myself to myself. If Papa or Mama found out they would be mad, and just beat me with their hands or belt. I was so scared and confused. I just did not know who I could tell or what to do.

Chapter 2

Missing Hugs

I just knew I couldn't let my parents know the truth about me urinating on myself in my sleep; it would get worse for me. The morning came and I had to get ready for school the next day. I quietly walked upstairs' I did not want my parent's to hear me. I took a hot shower, hurried up and put on clean clothes and acted as if nothing ever happened last night.

When I got at school, things didn't go well for me at all on that day. I was having serious trouble concentrating and really did not want to be at school on that day. I walked around in a daze all day, my mind was all confused. I never responded when the Teacher or the other kids would call my name in the classroom. I just couldn't stop thinking about what happen to me on that awful week of my parent's family reunion. The problems Mama and Papa put me through and the shame I felt. I do not understand why Mama or Papa didn't allowed me to be upstairs with the rest of their family. Mama and Papa really must be ashamed of me, that's the reason they made me stay downstairs.

School was over and I was planning in my head all day the right words to say to Mama and Papa when I saw them. No matter how hard I was thinking, my words just made no sense in my head. When I got home from school I wanted to sleep in my room and not end up sleeping in the basement again. It all depended on which one of parent's I would see first.

I got home and Papa was the first person I saw and my heartbeat speeded up. Papa came home early from work feeling sick. The sickness still did not stop Papa from having his liquor bottle on the table by him. I opened the door and walked into the living room where Papa was. I saw Papa sitting there in his favorite chair watching television.

First I thought, should I tell Papa what I was thinking about or Mama? I wasn't exactly sure what to do until Papa asked me a question and I was relieved he did. Papa said, "Penny what took you so long to get home from school anyway?" "Papa, I walked a different way home today, it took a little longer than I thought it would have been." Then I asked, "Papa can't I talk to you about something?" Papa said, "Penny hurry up, I'm watching TV what is it?" "Papa, I will be a good boy for you from now on, so that Mama and you will love and be proud of. I promise Papa, you will see that I will be a good boy."

Papa says, "What are you talking about, go put your books away, get out of my face don't you see I'm trying to watch TV. HUSH YOUR MOUTH Penny! Move out of my way you're blocking my view."

I ran upstairs; I heard the doorbell ring as I sat on my bed in my room. I put up my school books on the bed like I always did, every day. I walked back downstairs making sure I sat quietly on the couch in the living room waiting for dinner to be done. Papa's friend from work came by our house to give him his new work schedule. I listened to Papa and his friend from work laughing as they talked. I asked Papa if I could turn the station on the television. Papa ignored me and kept laughing and talking to his friend. I didn't think Papa would care if I turned on the television. Especially since Papa was busy talking to his friend.

Then Papa's friend that came over left our house. I knew already I was in trouble for opening my big mouth. Papa never permits anyone to talk to him or disturb him if he was watching his favorite television shows. How could I have been so stupid to disturb or ask Papa a question? I started feeling very nervous inside; I was not sure why Papa's friend left so quickly.

I could smell the strong odor from the liquor Papa was drinking and Papa just stared at me for a long time. I should have just sat there on the couch quiet like a mouse as they sneak into a room. Then Papa says "Penny, why are you always embarrassing me in front of my friends from work?" "Papa, I am sorry, I just thought I could turn the channel on the television since you were talking with your friend. I am sorry; I didn't mean to embarrass you. Papa, I am sorry." Papa yells; "Penny you know what your problem is you think too much for a little boy. You don't know how or when to keep your thinking or stupid mouth shut. I told your Mama I wish we would have had a girl it would have been much easier to raise a girl."

The tears started to roll down my cheeks as I listened to Papa. I just stared at Papa. I hushed my mouth and didn't say another word. I just waited for what Papa would say or do to me next. Papa says; "Penny the next time I or your Mama have any visitors in this house. It's best you go down stairs to your room in the basement. Penny, I want you to stay there until one of us tells you to come back upstairs." I was so scared, I quickly said; "Yes Sir Papa. I will go down in the basement like you told me." I didn't want to upset Papa any more than what he already was at me.

After I listened to what Papa said to me. I knew in my heart that I was not the child my Mama or Papa wanted to be born. There isn't a child I know or met in my lifetime they ever said before they are born; "Ok, I guess today is the day I will come into these people lives and world." How could I have been so stupid anyway? In my head, I thought Pee; you are always doing something wrong. Penny, you shouldn't have asked Papa anything at all about the television. What is wrong with me? Why are you so stupid Penny, as the bad thoughts just kept racing in my head? Then I yelled out loudly JUST HUSH YOUR MOUTH PENNY! STOP IT PEE!!!

Mama yells; "PEE, dinner is ready, come eat." I hesitated at first then I went and washed my hands in the bathroom. When I was finished I walked into the kitchen and sat down at the table quietly. Waiting quietly until Mama was done saying her prayer over the food like Mama always did. Which seem like the prayer took forever to me. I didn't understand how my Parents could pray with their tongues then speak words out of her mouth that would cut my heart like a knife the way they always did.

I was starving on that night and so excited too, just to be sitting at the table. I was also glad that Mama let me come upstairs to the table to eat at least for a second. This was going to be the first night I would get to sleep back in my own bed in my room. I was hungry and was looking forward to a good dinner at the table with Mama and Papa. Finally things would get back to normal. I could just go back to disappearing at the table with Mama and Papa like I always did. The meal Mama made that day was all of the favorite's foods. Mama cooked fried chicken, macaroni with cheese, mashed potatoes and cornbread.

I really thought it was going to a great night for me. I watched Mama put four pieces of the fried chicken on a platter in the middle of the table. Then Papa quickly grabs the platter and puts three pieces of the fried chicken on his plate. There was only one piece of the fried chicken left. I grabbed the last piece of fried chicken and handed it to my Mama. Papa always made sure if there was any food on the table he would get the food he wanted first. Mama and I would just eat what Papa did not want. I did not speak a word; I just watched Mama and Papa eat.

It was so silent in the room it bothered me. Mama or Papa weren't talking to each other either on that night as we sat at the dining table. I just hushed my mouth and waited. Thinking to myself, what is going to happen to me next? Something didn't feel right in my stomach at the table on that night. I finally got up enough nerve and asked Mama "did everybody have a goodtime at the Family reunion?" It was quiet for a minute until Papa yells and said to me; "You almost ruined the family reunion with your big mouth Penny." "Papa, I don't understand how or what I did wrong. I stayed downstairs in the basement like you both told me to do."

Mama just stares at me like she was disgusted with me. I could see the hate in my Mama's and Papa's eyes on that night as they both kept staring at me. Mama reaches into her pocket and pulls out some of her pills, takes one as I watch her. Then Mama gets up from the table, walks over to me with this big smile on her face. I never even seen it coming and Mama slaps my face with her hand. My head turns from Mama slapping my face so hard. Then Mama takes her other hand and slaps the other side of my face as hard as she could. I put my hands on the sides of my face as the tears run down my cheek. Then Mama says "Pee, you had problems the entire time my family was visiting our home. You should have hushed your mouth like me and Papa told you to do. Do you think I and your Papa are stupid Pee?"

"I'm sorry Mama for talking back to you," as I cry "Mama, I am sorry." There was a silence in the room as Papa just stared at me. I sat there waiting for Papa to take his hands and slap both sides of my face again. Until Papa stood up and walked over to me and said, "Why is it that you don't know how to hush your mouth Penny? You told me Penny, you're going to be a good boy, isn't that what you told me Penny?" Then Mama interrupted Papa and said; "Is that what Pee said?" I started crying louder until Papa says; "HUSH YOUR MOUTH PEE!! You could never be a good boy. Pee, you disgust me and you have ruined me and your Mother's dinner for tonight."

Mama got up and left the dining table mad at me. I was hoping it was all over since Mama had left the table, but I should have known better. Papa always has the last word; it was never over with Papa. Papa kept staring at me. I knew in my mind he was thinking about what he was going to do to me next. I kept looking down at the floor. I never allow my eyes to meet Papa's eyes or my head to look in his direction. Papa always told me if I looked into his eyes I was disrespecting him.

I was too afraid to say another word or eat or do anything at all. I sat there with my entire body shaking from head to toe. I continued to keep my head down, looking at the floor, and not at Papa. Then again, I didn't have to speak because Papa had the last words anyway. I knew already the words that were coming next out of Papa mouth. Papa said; "Penny go grab your blanket from upstairs. You will be sleeping downstairs for the night for upsetting your Mama at the dinner table."

I was too scared to ask any questions. Then I said, "Papa, may I please be excused from the table, Sir?" Papa said; "Penny boy, you already were excused from the table. You're spoiling my supper, HUSH YOUR MOUTH! GET OUT OF MY SIGTH NOW

BEFORE I HURT YOU BAD." I ran upstairs fast with my entire body shaking, the tears from my eyes hitting every step I took. I grabbed my blanket quick off the bed that I thought I was going to be sleeping on. I ran back downstairs to the basement as fast as my legs would take me.

I was used to being in the basement; it was the only place that I could be safe and far away from Mama and Papa. It was another night that I had to survive. I just was not sure how, besides; I was only a little boy. I went to bed hungry and scared with my body shaking all over on that miserable night. My mind was blank. I just did know how to think or what to do. I just didn't know how to make myself disappear forever. I wish I did. Besides, what really was I going to do anyway? Nobody would have ever believed me anyway.

I started talking out loud to myself again. My mind I heard, "Pee just run away somewhere, just leave. Then Penny said; stay quiet Pee, HUSH YOUR MOUTH!" All those crazy thoughts started racing through my mind fast as a car on a speed track racing all at once. I thought, what is wrong with me? I am losing my mind. I do not understand what I did to be down here in this basement again. I also was not sure how long my parents were going to leave me down here in this dirty basement this time? Then, in my head I disappeared. I saw myself at the playground having fun and I dozed off to sleep.

Only to wake up the next morning with my pajamas soaked with my urine I really didn't understand and felt too embarrassed to tell anyone about what was happening to me. Papa also told me; "Penny you beta not ever tell anyone, or I will hurt you bad." It seemed as I grew older the urinating on myself got worst. It kept happening more frequently. I eventually just got used to it. I just kept hiding all my clothes that were wet from urine from my Mama and Papa.

The basement became the only safe place for me to be, or eat, or sleep. I also knew I had to get away from Papa. I make sure I stayed out of Mama's and Papa's sight. I spent many birthdays in that cold, dirty, nasty basement as I grew older, and angrier about what was happening to me. I go the school and come back home and go back down to the basement. I was learning absolutely nothing in school,

I could not concentrate. All that was on my mind was why are my parents treating me this way?

I am fifteen years old now and about to turn sixteen. How was I going to explain my crappy messed up life to anyone? Every night, when I go to sleep, I urinate on myself. Nobody would ever understand me anyway and would laugh at me. I didn't understand either, it was too embarrassing, and I was confused. I was told by Mama and Papa never to invite any of my friends from school to the house. I had no friends to invite to the house, so it didn't bother me. I could not have friends over anyway with Papa's temper. I really didn't want anyone to know or see how I was being treated.

Every day I just kept waiting to be squashed like a spider walking across the floor. I did know this one boy at school named Chad that went to my school. I think the only reason Chad spoke to me was because he felt sorry for me. I hated every day I had to return back to that miserable house with Mama and Papa. I always would try to sneak back into the house quietly. No way did I want to upset Mama or Papa when I got in from school.

It was a strange day for me; I was so used to being in the basement it didn't matter to me anymore. The boy Pee or Penny was gone. He disappeared a long time ago. I did not even know who I was anymore, I was so confused, so scared. I knew other children do not live the way I was living. I started accepting and believing in my heart my messed-up life was the way it was supposed to be. I spent many birthdays down in the basement, and holidays too. I didn't expect a birthday cake or ice cream or anything from Mama or Papa. I was lucky if I was given food to eat. I also learned the hard way not to ask Papa or Mama for anything. I noticed how my Parents stopped talking to each other; or me anymore. It was better this way for me; this was going to be the only way that I would survive living in that house. Papa was drunk all the time and Mama made sure she stayed out of Papa's way. To be totally honest with you, it didn't bother me at all that Mama or Papa didn't have any talks with me. I really didn't want to talk to them anymore. I kept thinking what I did to cause all this to happen to me?

I woke up early on that Saturday morning, I was excited. Today is the big day that I turned sixteen; it was my birthday. I walked upstairs from the basement, took a shower, and then I walked into the dining room. Mama was already sitting at the table with this look on her face. I sat down, said "Good morning, Mama."

I didn't expect Mama to say to me; Happy Birthday Pee. I knew nobody cared it was my birthday anymore. I was lucky to be alive to see another birthday in that house. Mama started right away on me just as I thought she would. Mama says; "Pee I know you're sixteen now, that does not mean you're going to be coming in this house anytime you want. Sixteen years old does not make you a man." "Yes Mama, I will not be coming in the house late tonight." Mama was still sitting at the table by herself as I left the house.

My one friend named Chad from school had a little party for me in his parent's garage on Saturday night. It was really just Chad and a couple girls he knew; we all were drinking and getting high. I thought everything was going good until I started getting drunk. I just kept drinking for the rest of the night until I couldn't think or walk straight. I lost track of the time and totally forgot about everything. I forgot about the time Mama told me to be in the house.

Time went by so fast on that night. I asked my friend Chad, "What time is it now? I have to get home." My friend Chad said; "It's three o'clock in the morning, man." I hurried up and put on my coat; then I ran home as fast as I could. I didn't even say goodbye to Chad that night, or thank you. I never thought I was going to make it to the front steps at the house. All the lights were turned off but the front door was unlocked. I thought maybe if I'm quiet Mama or Papa won't hear me sneaking back into the house. I was wrong. I quietly open the door and took one step into the living room. There stood Mama waiting in the living room and staring at my face.

I knew what was coming next when Mama says; "Pee, you're a big man now that you turned sixteen; you can come and go as you please." "No Mama, I lost track of the time. I couldn't remember the time you told me to come home." Mama said to me; "Pee, you lost a lot of things; you make no sense, Pee. How could you be born so stupid that you can't even read a clock? I told your Papa I wish I had a girl! Boys are nothing but problems; they always have trouble telling the time. Your Papa wanted a girl too, you know what I think Pee?"

Missing Hugs

I didn't want to answer Mama, but I knew if I didn't, she was going to slap my face and make a lot of noise. I didn't want Papa to wake up from his sleep, it would be worst. I said; "No Mama, what is it that you think?" Then Mama said; "I think you will never be a good boy or a good man. You will always be stupid Pee, just a stupid boy that nobody wants around. All you will ever be is a stupid boy that can't even read a clock at the age sixteen."

Mama's words cut sharp like a razor that night and went straight through my heart again. I couldn't bear to hear anymore of Mama's razor sharp words, it hurt my feelings too much. I asked Mama "Please may I go now to my room downstairs? I will be quiet." Mama said; "Yeah, go to your room in the basement, then pray hard. I don't tell your Papa the time you came into this house tonight Mr. Big Man Pee."

I quietly walked down to my room in the basement. When I got down there, I was afraid to fall asleep. I kept thinking, what if Mama went upstairs and told Papa the time I came home? I finally dozed off to sleep, only to be awakened by Papa standing over me, laughing. Papa yells; "PENNY GET YOUR BUTT UP NOW." I just looked up at Papa standing there, I was half sleep. I kept hoping it was a bad dream, but it wasn't.

As soon Papa started talking I could smell the alcohol on his breath. I kept thinking about a way I could run past Papa; then I thought, what if he catches me? Then Papa said; "Penny, three o'clock in the morning is early for a big man like you." I wasn't sure how to answer Papa; he was being sarcastic; so I just stayed quiet. Then Papa says; "Why does this sixteen year old boy room smell like piss if he is such a big man?"

I realized that I had forgotten to do the laundry the day before. The entire basement smelled like urine. I couldn't believe that I forgot to do the laundry. Papa says; "PENNY, BIG MAN ARE YOU DEAF? ANSWER ME NOW." I got out of the bed and looked away from Papa with both of my legs shaking. I was so afraid. Before I realized it, I started urinating all over myself as I was standing there. Papa starts laughing at me then he says; "You're not a big man now that you're sixteen. You're still Penny, a little Pee boy. Or maybe you're just a little girl that doesn't know how to go to the bathroom and needs to be potty trained by their Mama."

Then Papa burst out laughing as loud as he could and walked back upstairs. After Papa left, I was mad and felt ashamed. Why does He treat me so badly? What Father in this world would talk or treat their child the way Papa treated me. From then on, I fathered myself and accepted the fact the man I called Papa, didn't love or care about me. I was living in a house with people that could care less if I lived or died.

I wasn't the child they wanted in their lives and I knew I had to get out of that house. Mama and Papa didn't try to pretend they wanted or loved me. I felt all mixed up, confused in my head. My sad reality was I was a troubled boy and was going through life with no purpose or love. I will never meet their expectations to be that good boy they would love. They both told me they didn't want a boy like me.

I was angry and made up my mind after Papa spoke those hurtful words to me. On that morning, the way he did that, my life was going to be different, starting today. My plan was to get out of their basement and move far away from Mama and Papa forever. I never thought for a second my parents had some plans of their own for me. My main problem was I just never knew what Papa or Mama would say or do to me next. Then I thought, it really doesn't matter to me anymore. Whatever Mama or Papa decided to do to me wouldn't be worse than what they have already done to me. I still kept remembering how Papa and Mama had the nerve to say, "Say a prayer." On the same day I was hungry, Papa didn't let me eat. I never understood how my own parent could say, "say your prayers." Then those same parents, after they are done with their superficial prayer, hate their own child sitting across from them at the same table.

I didn't know who these two people were anymore. I thought; why was I born to a Mother or Father that did not want a child anyway? The only thoughts on my mind were how long it will be before I lost my mind or life. Papa always found some awful way to humiliate me. I never understood how people can laugh at or about a person's pain. There was no reason for me to be around, or living in that house. It did not take long before I questioned my own existence.

I started believing I wasn't important to anyone. I was treated like garbage. Actually, my parents gave the garbage more attention than they ever gave me. Often, I would try to fall asleep and neither of them would even speak a word to me. If you live a certain way, or told you are trash long enough, you start to believe it must be true. I knew trash was who I was every day; I believed it was true. Trash is what I was. I kept waiting for Mama or Papa to say to me they didn't want trash or me in their house anymore. In my heart I knew that day was approaching me fast.

Chapter 3

LOVE IS THE INGREDIENT MISSING

The morning came. Papa was drunk again. Papa couldn't wait to tell Mama the news about me urinating on myself out of fear last night. Papa didn't tell Mama the reason why, or about how scared I really was last night. There we sat, Papa, Mama, and I at the breakfast table. Mama knew I was starting to act very different. I wouldn't even look at her or Papa if they spoke to me anymore. I was fed up with the way they both were treating me. I didn't know what to do that would help me get away from them. I just didn't think things could get any worst for me than they already were.

That morning things got worse for me as soon as Mama opened her mouth to talk. Mama says; "Pee I heard about last night." "Please excuse me Papa and Mama, I have to leave for school. I'm late." Papa said; "What's the hurry Penny? I know why your Mama said your name should be Pee." Before I knew it, I stood up, left the table, and ran out the front door. Mama was saying something as I was leaving and I didn't listen to her words, or Papa's. I knew their tongues were razor sharp. The only way I could protect my heart from getting cut deeper was to run out of their house.

I thought as I was walking to school that my life was nothing but a big joke. It made me feel sad as I thought about the way Papa had made fun of me at the table that morning. I arrived at school and acted like nothing ever happened to me. I always pretended if I was at school. Only there was no school. We were on Christmas break from school. It was Christmas Eve.

I was trying real hard to keep all the bad thoughts out of my head about what happened to me. The bad thoughts kept coming back no matter how hard I tried. I would close my eyes and I would see Papa standing there laughing at me and buckling up his pants. Then I would hear the words my Papa would say; "Hush Your Mouth, Penny."

They told Papa he had to work on the day of Christmas Eve. I was glad. Mama was busy cooking in the kitchen baking desserts for the holiday. I got this big idea that I should try to help Mama before Papa comes home from work. I thought this will give me and Mama a chance to talk. I never talk to Mama alone anymore Papa never let that happen. Papa always told me; "Men don't have any business in a kitchen, boy. Leave the cooking to the woman." I definitely didn't want Papa to catch me in the kitchen at all. If Papa caught me in the kitchen, I would be yelled at and sent to the basement on Christmas. Christmas was not about me. Nothing was about me. I just stood there watching Mama prepare the food. They never cared about anything they said or did to me. I was not the child they wanted.

I walked in the kitchen and I asked Mama this question. "Mama, do you think Papa loves or cares about me?" Mama acted like she didn't hear me and didn't answer my question. I was hoping Mama would answer my question about Papa, so I asked again. "Tell me Mama, does Papa or you love or care about me at all?" Mama said, "HUSH YOUR MOUTH!! Pee, it's your fault we talk the way we do to you. You're a child and you are supposed to be seen and not heard. Learn to keep your big mouth shut."

I asked, "What way you're talking about. Mama, I do not know what you're talking about." I never got an answer by Mama. Instead, Mama quickly changed the subject. I watched as Mama tasted the apple filling she made. Mama says to me; "Pee I think there's definitely something missing in this apple filling for these pies. I have to check the oven to see how my pie is doing. It's Christmas, I have to be ready for Christmas before your Papa gets home or there is going to be trouble. Pee, look on that shelf. Grab for me the bag of sugar out of the cabinet. This apple filling has no taste. It's bland. Something is missing. This filling doesn't have the main ingredients it needs. I can tell by the taste."

I looked down at the sugar and Mama snatches it out of my hand, and poured the entire bag of sugar in her apple filling. I still stood there waiting patiently for Mama to answer my question. Then I watched Mama taste the apple filling again. Mama says to me; "Pee, that is what it was missing. I forgot the main ingredients." I just stared at Mama like she was crazy until these words just came out of my mouth. I yelled "Mama, LOVE IS THE MISSING INGREDIENT! That is what's missing!"

I walked away and Mama threw her cast iron frying pan at me. It hit me in the back of my head as I walked out the door. I was thinking in my heart how much I hated the day I was born. The back of my head was hurting and bleeding. Even so, I was not going back into that house. I was so mad. I decided to walk to the park my friend Chad usually hung out in. I started walking over to talk to my friend Chad. The anger in my heart had my entire body shaking. I was trying to figure out a place for me to stay. There was no way I was going to show my feelings to Chad. So as I got closer to Chad, I put on a mask. A mask just like the ones children would wear on Halloween. Then I said, "Chad, my Mama and Papa told me to leave the house. They are getting everything ready for a big Christmas surprise for me." I lied and told Chad, "I can't wait to go back home." My friend Chad said to me; "Your parents must love you a lot, dude." People that knew me started calling me "P" as I grew older. "Yeah, Chad you're right, my Mama and Papa really do love me very much."

Inside my heart, I knew none of that was the truth. How could I have told anyone the real truth? I felt too ashamed. Papa had me convinced that nobody would care or believe me anyway. I had no choice other than to leave the park and return back to the insanity in that awful house. I couldn't think of anywhere else I could go to stay or live. As I was walking on my way back home, I saw Papa's car sitting in front of his liquor store. I didn't want Papa to see me, so I quickly crossed the street. Papa got out of his car staggering drunk. Holding on to the side of his car with every step he took. Papa opens the passenger side door and I saw this lady walk out of the liquor store. I watch the lady get into Papa's car and saw Papa smile. I knew the lady wasn't my Mama, because I had just left the house. Mama was still in the kitchen standing there when I left, cooking.

Then Papa turned the car and starts driving toward the corner where I was standing. I thought Papa would see me if I ran from the spot where I was hiding. It was too late for me to run. Papa was turning the corner fast. He saw me. I stood there shaking, knowing I was big trouble. Papa stopped the car and yelled out the car window at me. "Penny, stay there until I park the car. I have to talk to you. Don't you move."

Before Papa got the car in park my feet wanted to move. I knew Papa was drunk and it really wouldn't matter anyway if I moved. Papa gets out of his car and starts walking toward me. I could smell the alcohol and my heart was speeding up faster and faster. Then Papa was standing right in front of me. I quickly put my head down. I dared not look into Papa eyes. I just "Hushed my mouth," and waited for Papa to speak. Then Papa says; "I know Penny you must of saw my lady friend in the car. I am giving her a ride home. Her car broke down." I continued to stay quiet, looking down at the ground. I knew if I spoke any words it would just make Papa mad at me. I didn't want to get hit by Papa on Christmas Eve, or at all.

Papa yells "Penny, you beta not go home and tell your Mama you saw me at all. You wouldn't want to upset your Mama again like you did last time on Christmas Eve. Be a good Penny and HUSH YOUR MOUTH!" I shook my head no and Papa walked away, laughing at me. This was the day I realize it's not just me Papa don't love, he doesn't love Mama, either. I walked back to that miserable house as fast as I could. I got back home and sat down in the living room. I did not turn on the television. I knew any second that Papa was going to be walking through the front door.

Then Papa walks in laughing, as he enters the house. Papa looks over at me, then smiled and never spoke a word to me. I heard Mama ask Papa; "How was work?" Papa says, "It was a hard day. A couple of guys didn't bother showing up for work, I had to work twice as hard." Papa always knew what to say to Mama that would keep her mouth shut from asking too many questions. Then Mama yells,

"Pee, Dinner Ready." I washed my hands. Mama had all the food on the table when I walked into the kitchen. Papa got done with saying his fake prayer finally.

There I sat again, watching and listening to Mama and Papa talk on Christmas Eve. They both acted as if I was invisible again and never spoke a word to me, not even Merry Christmas. I got tired of listening to them talk to each other. I asked if could leave the table, stood up, and left the food on the plate. I went back to my room downstairs in the basement and sat on the blanket on the floor. I had already gotten used to Mama and Papa not getting me presents or anything. I waited until they both went to sleep that night and I snuck out of the house.

My plan was to sneak back into the house before they woke up and realized I was gone. I just wanted to walk around, get away from them and that basement. The bad feelings kept racing in my head about my parents and the bad way they were treating me. It made my head hurt worse and the pain in my head was already indescribable. I wanted to cry, but the tears never formed in my eyes. It didn't matter how hard I tried to cry.

The only thing I felt in my heart was hurt and rage. I knew I had to get away from them before it was too late for me. I kept wishing I was a bird and I knew a bird could fly and escape to safety. Deep inside my heart, I knew that I would have to go back. There was no way out. I arrived back to the house, quietly walked back down to the basement. I tried to fall asleep but couldn't so I just sat on my blanket on the floor.

I stayed up the entire night just waiting for Papa to come down the stairs to yell at me. It didn't matter how much I tried to forget about what was happening to me, it was all I could think about. It bothered me more that night as I started remembering the times in the basement. Papa would be standing in front of me buckling up his pants when I woke up. Mama would never believe me and I knew she would take sides with Papa. It was like I was expected to just accept whatever happened to me and never question Papa. There wasn't anybody in this world I trusted enough to tell. I just "hushed my mouth." Papa and Mama had already told me if I opened my mouth to tell people; they would both would say I was lying. The truth was, Mama always protected Papa and Papa always protected Mama. Nobody protected me. Nobody! Why would I cry? It never eased my pain or changed my situation it just made me hate more.

I felt that I had absolutely nothing in this world to look forward to or live for. Every day, I was living with two people that hated me and did not want me around. Still, I was supposed to be happy living in a situation like I was. I couldn't take it anymore and I was determined to do something about it. School had started back after the Christmas break was over. There were a bunch of new kids in my class. I was just glad to get out of that house and away from the craziness. The less I saw them or was at home, I knew, the better it would be for me.

One of the new dudes in my class was my friend Chad. He walked over to me and said; "Pee, There's a big party me and my boys are throwing tonight. You should come by the house, Pee, tonight." I told Chad that I'd definitely be there. It was time to go back to that miserable house and I just wanted to change clothes as fast as possible. I went home and didn't even care about eating dinner that night. I was too excited about the party. I quickly changed my clothes and left walking to Chad's house before Mama or Papa even knew I was ever home.

When I got there you could smell the alcohol and pot as soon as you walked through the garage doors. The smell didn't bother me. I was use to the alcohol smell from the house I had been living in. When Chad sees me he says; "Glad you came to the party man. You ready to get high?" I never smoked pot. Beer I had already tried. "Yeah Chad, I am ready to get high. Let's do this." Chad handed me the pot and I started to smoke it fast. I coughed a lot.

As time passed and I drank more alcohol, all those bad feelings I was having in my head about Mama and Papa were gone. Nothing mattered to me on that night. I just wanted to drink as much alcohol as possible. Chad wanted to introduce me to some girls that were at the party. Always, I was shy went it came to talking to girls. Then Chad says; "C'mon Pee, there's this girl I want you to meet. I know you're going to like her man, she's real cool."

I walked over with Chad into his house where there was a bunch of girls just hanging out talking with each other. Chad and I walk

LOVE IS THE INGREDIENT MISSING

over in front of this one girl. Chad stops and says "Pee, this is my girl Trina." I stood there, not knowing what to say to this girl. Then Trina says to me "What's up? How you doing Pee?" "Fine, Trina" I said, and then Chad and I walked back into Chad living room. I was just watching everybody dancing having a goodtime, until I started feeling paranoid. The party at Chad house seemed like it lasted forever to me on that night. I was glad it did, because I didn't want to go back to the house I was living in anyway. Everyone was leaving except for me; I was the last person to leave Chad party on that night. I asked Chad what time it was, I had to get home before my parents woke up. Chad says; "Man, its five o'clock in the morning." It can't be. Are you kidding me? I have to leave Chad, before Mama and Papa get up.

Then Chad says, "Just stay here tonight, you're old enough to stay out late. You're not a baby. Why are you all nervous about the time anyway?" "Chad, you don't understand, man. If I don't get my butt home before they wake up there's going to be big problems for me." Chad says; "I stop letting my parents tell me what to do and how to live. I'm eighteen years old. You will be eighteen in a few months. Don't worry about what your Mama or Papa think." "Chad if you were me. You would understand why I have to leave," and I left.

When I got home, Mama and Papa were still sound asleep. That was what they wanted me to think. I went downstairs, sat on the blanket in the basement, and then fell asleep. I was drunk. When I woke up, it was four o'clock in the afternoon, the next day. My clothes were soaked with urine because of me urinating on myself again. I had to figure out some way to sneak upstairs, and take a shower before Mama or Papa saw me. Papa was gone and Mama was in the kitchen.

I walked upstairs, quietly took a shower, and put on clean clothes. I walked back upstairs into the kitchen. Mama was sitting at the table with this serious look on her face and Papa wasn't home yet. I asked Mama; "Is Papa still at work?" Mama said, "I don't know, he didn't come home last night at all." "Mama, maybe he had to work a double shift because someone didn't show up for work again." Mama says; "Pee, what Papa does is not your business! Worry about where you were last night not Papa." "I was at a party at my friend's house, Mama. I just lost track of the time." Mama says; "You are getting out of control, Pee. You think you're grown. I always knew in my heart you were going to be a problem. Papa and I thought it would be better for you to stay in the room in the basement. This way you would be out of our sight and out of our way."

Before I knew it, I said; "Mama what about all those times Papa comes down to the basement. The times Papa is buckling up his pants when I wake up? Are you sleeping or awake?" Mama yells; "I know it's time for you to be out on your own. Stop lying on your Papa. Pee, you will be eighteen in a few months." I started begging Mama; "Please I'm sorry it won't happen again. I didn't know how late it was when I got home. Please Mama, I beg you! Do not tell Papa what I said, I am sorry!"

Mama says to me; "I know it won't happen again, not in my house. Get your stuff Pee, and get out of this house! I want you out of here before your Papa gets back home." "Mama, what are you talking about? I have nowhere to stay or go." I was surprised and never thought the day would come that Mama would say those words to me. Then Mama yells, "We NEVER wanted YOU! GET OUT of this house before I hurt you myself."

I just looked at Mama and went downstairs grab a few clothes and rolled them up in the blanket. A thought came in my mind; before I leave there is one thing I have to tell Mama. I walk back upstairs and said; "Mama you know I don't have anyone or anywhere to go. Then you tell me to get out of your house 'before you hurt me.' Mama, I'm only seventeen, I don't have a family like you and Papa. How am I supposed to live?"

Mama never spoke a word back to me, she just ignored me. "Mama, you're right, this has never been my house. I will never be that child you or Papa will ever love. I know you and Papa were always ashamed of me. It's ok, Mama, because I feel ashamed of you and Papa, too. I know that was the reason you both would always send me downstairs to live in the basement. You let me grow up in that dirty, cold basement. Many nights, I had no food and woke up to Papa's laughter as I watch him buckling up his pants."

LOVE IS THE INGREDIENT MISSING

Mama yells; "Hush your mouth Pee." I kept talking, "I don't understand why this is happening to me. I have always tried to be a good boy. I'm a child that nobody loves or wants around. How could you have not heard or known Mama? Papa was not quiet walking down to the basement. Tell me how come you never try to stop Papa from hurting me down in that basement? I tried so hard to be a child that you and Papa would be proud of and love. I still remember Mama, the day you made all those pies on Christmas day. Mama you were so proud of your pies and said there was still something missing."

Mama just stares at me and said; "You're crazy Pee! Get out of this house and never come back." My reply to Mama was; "I don't understand why Papa or you want me to think I am crazy. Love has always been the missing ingredient in my life. Love is the missing ingredient in this miserable house!!" Mama yells; "GET OUT OF THIS HOUSE. WE NO LONGER HAVE A SON NAMED PENNY OR PEE."

I walked out of the house as fast as I could and never went back there to live, ever again. I ran outside and down the street as far as my legs would take me away from Mama and Papa's house. I had to stop running to sit down on a bench at the park to think. I was tired from running so much. The first thought that came to my mind was, I'm finally free from that basement and the misery I was living in.

I decided to walk over to Chad house to ask him if I could stay at his house. At least until I could find a place of my own to stay. As I was walking fear came into my heart, all I kept thinking about was what if Mama tells Papa about the words I said when he comes home. I dismissed that thought quick; I couldn't be worried about what Papa thought. I had bigger problems than that for the night. I didn't have any money or place to stay for the night. My only belongings when I left my parents house were the clothes on my back, also a dirty blanket to sleep on.

I got to Chad's house and knocked on his door as hard as I could. Chad opened the door, I asked; "Can I talk to you man? In private." Chad came outside on his front porch and asked me; "What's up Pee?" "My parents threw me out of their house. I don't have any family living in this town, not sure if you can help me out or not. Do

Missing Love Child

you think I could stay with you until I can figure out somewhere else to stay?" I waited for Chad to answer, then he said; "Pee, you could stay here. It's cool with me."

When I got inside Chad house, I asked Chad where I should sleep. "Do you have a basement? I brought my blanket." Chad said; "What are you talking about a basement. Dude, you can sleep in my living room on the couch, it's big enough." I didn't know what to say. I was thinking it's been years since I slept in a room. I was shocked by Chad response. Then Chad says; "I don't know what happened to you, man. I don't need to know, it's not my business." "I'm never going back there Chad. It does not matter what happens to me. I am done with all that crazy stuff and that crazy house." Chad said to me; "forget about that stuff man. Let's go hangout tonight." "Yeah, "C," let's go." Then we left. I had no idea what my new life was going to be like after I moved into Chad house. I knew it couldn't be any worse than my life has been living with Papa in their house.

Chad liked to party all the time. He always had something we could get high on. I started meeting up with a lot of people at these different parties Chad and I were always going to. At the parties, I was getting high all the time. It helped me ease the deep pain I had in my heart. Weeks went by. I didn't hear anything from my Papa or Mama. I was so glad. I thought it was over. I could have made a life for myself. At least that is what I thought until I started hearing from people on the streets. Papa was out looking for me and asking if people saw me. I asked Chad not to tell Papa if he saw him on the streets where I was staying. I didn't trust Papa. I knew he was crazy. I was afraid of what he might do to me if he found me. After I heard Papa was looking for me, I started looking over my shoulder everywhere I went. I couldn't go anywhere without somebody telling me "Pee you beta watch your back."

Chapter 4

LOVE MADE ME BEAT YOU

I was living constantly in fear even though I wasn't living in Mama and Papa's house anymore. It was nuts. My grades in school were failing. I decided to drop out of school. I kept missing too many days. I couldn't concentrate or fake it anymore. I was nervous all the time. I kept thinking about what if Mama or Papa found me. What would I do if they came to school or embarrass me or cause a big scene?

My friend Chad and I were sitting in his living room just hanging out, watching television. Only to be disturbed by a loud knock on the front door. At first, we just looked at each other. Then Chad walks over to the window and looks out from behind the curtain and says; "Pee, that's your father out there, you should go hide before I open the door." I ran downstairs into Chad basement and stayed very quiet. Then I heard the door open and Papa's voice saying; "Have you seen Penny, Chad?" Chad quickly says; "No, I haven't seen him." Then Papa says; "If you see Penny, tell him I got something for him and I want to talk to him."

Papa left, then Chad quickly closes the door and yells down the stairs to me; "Your Father gone, Pee. You can come back upstairs now." I went back upstairs feeling scared inside, then I said; Chad, I hope you didn't tell him I was living here." Chad gets mad at me and says; "Dude why do you think I would do that! You need to stop running from your Papa, anyway. It's not your fault you were told to leave their house." I started thinking and told Chad; "You're right, it's not. It's their fault they threw me out into the streets." Then we both went to sleep for the night.

The next day came. I walked into the kitchen. Chad asked me to run down to the store to pick up a gallon of milk. I put on my coat and left. I had to cross the street and walk through the park. The park was empty. It was early in the morning and it was quiet. I walked faster. I didn't see anybody hanging in the park that morning as I was walking. I continued walking fast to the store then I heard this voice from a distance yell; "Penny don't you move stay right there."

The voice sounded familiar. I knew inside my heart it was the voice of Papa. I stood there with my legs frozen, hoping please, let it be anybody else in this world except for Papa. I kept looking around. I didn't see anyone until I felt this tap on my shoulder. I turned around and it was Papa, looking straight into my face. I quickly put my head down and looked at the ground out of fear.

Papa says to me; "Penny where you been hiding all these days?" "Papa, I just been staying with some friends. Mama told me to leave the house; didn't she tell you what happened that night?" Papa says; "That isn't the way I heard it went on that night. Your Mama told me that you stayed out all night long and disrespected her on the night you left."

I attempted to tell Papa that was not the way it happened, that it was not true. It all happened so fast before I even had a chance to say a word, Papa swings at me and punches me in my mouth. I never even saw his fist coming toward my face. "Please wait Papa!" I begged and cried. Papa says to me; "Penny you will know you're not a man by the time I'm finished beating the lies out of you."

Papa punches me again in my face; both my mouth and nose were bleeding. I dropped to my knees and put my hands over my mouth and nose, trying to stop the bleeding. From my nose and mouth streams of blood kept falling to the ground. I begged; "Papa, PLEASE PAPA PLEASE!! Don't hit me anymore." Papa spit on me and says; "You better never tell anyone I hit you. Or you will wish you weren't born at all. Remember I will find you again, it does not matter where you hide." I yelled out again; "Please!" Papa says; "Hush your mouth Penny! Love is why I am beating you," and then

Papa spits on me again. Then Papa took his foot and kicked me on the side of my head until I passed out. All I saw was blood before the darkness took me. Papa walked away and left me there in the park lying in my own blood and his spit.

I started to get worried thinking to myself, Chad how could I have been so stupid asking Penny to go to the store by himself. Penny wasn't back from the store I decided to put on my coat and go look for Penny. I knew it doesn't take that long to go to the store. I felt something was wrong. I hurried up and ran across the street. I got to the park and I saw someone lying there on the ground from a distance. I started running fast as I could. As I got closer I could see that the person on the ground was Penny lying in his own blood. I yelled out; "Help me! Please somebody do something! Please help!"

A man ran over and asked me what happen to this guy lying here? Then the same man called for an ambulance to come. The ambulance arrived fast. I decided to ride in the ambulance with Penny to the hospital. I thought Penny was going to die on that night.

When I woke up; I was at the hospital. I saw Chad and the police sitting in the room. "What happened?" I asked. "And why are the police here in my room?" C says "Penny you know why. Tell them what happened to you." "Chad, I don't know what you're talking about or who the man that did this to me was. I think it was just a man trying to rob me at the park; that is all I can remember." Chad looked over at me, angry, and walked out of the room upset.

The police officer asked me; "Did you see the man's face at all that tried to rob you?" I answered; "No I did not. I never saw the man before at the park." The Police officer said; "If you can remember anything at all, please call me." The police officer left the room. They kept me for a few days at the hospital until I was ready to leave. Chad and Trina, the girl I met at Chad party, came by often to see me at the hospital. Everyday Chad would come visit me at the hospital. Chad didn't talk to me much anymore after that day I told the police I didn't know who beat me up. Mama never came by the hospital to see me at all. I know the hospital called Mama to let her know I was at the hospital.

I knew the person that beat me up in the park was Papa. I just didn't know how to tell anyone else that Papa was the man who beat me in the name of love this way. Depression was overcoming me. I started to cry all the time at the hospital. I kept thinking about what I was going to do when the time came for me to be discharged from the hospital. Papa would find me again. It didn't matter to him where I went.

The Doctor told me I was going to be discharged from the hospital and asked me where I would be living. I told the Doctor with my friend Chad and his family. I knew it would be safe for me to stay at Chad house. Trina and Chad came to the hospital the day I was being discharged. I was glad, and wasn't about to walk out of the hospital alone after what happened to me at the park.

When we got back to Chad house; Trina left to go back to her own house. Chad says; "Penny, man, I have to talk to you." I asked Chad; "What is it you need to talk to me about?" Chad replied; "I can't keep dealing with the crap your parents are doing to you. You should have told the people at the hospital what really happened." I said, "Chad, I am still alive. Everything is ok. Papa beat me that way because he loves me. That's what Papa said." Chad yells; "PENNY, you're losing your freaking mind! That is not love."

I just stared at Chad. I was mad after he said those words to me. Chad was mad at me too, and then Chad walked out of his house. After Chad left, I sat down in the chair at the kitchen table and thought. Chad didn't have a right to talk to me like that. I made up my mind. I was going to talk to Chad as soon as he returned home. Chad did return, and my words to him were; "Chad, you don't know what you're talking about concerning my family." Then Chad yells at me; "Penny, then you should go live back with them if they love you so much. Just keep putting up with the crap they are doing to you if you really believe that is love."

I stayed quiet. Chad was right. I was so confused; I knew in my heart I was wrong. I didn't know what I was saying or thinking anymore. After Papa beat me up, I started feeling like I was losing my mind. I wanted to forget that day ever happened to me.

Trina, now Chad's girlfriend, was having a big party and I was invited. I took a shower and got dressed. I left Chad's house to go over to Trina's party. My plan was to get over to Trina's place before everyone else arrived. I wanted to spend some time talking to Trina, this way we could get to know each other better.

I was two blocks from Trina's place as I ran across the street looking over my shoulder; thinking about what Papa did to me as I walked past the park. I passed a grocery store on Trina's block and this lady came walking out the store's front door. I couldn't believe it; it was my Mama coming out of the store. I ran over to her and asked; "Mama, how is everything going?" Mama didn't answer me or even look in my direction. Then Mama walked by me fast, as if she didn't know who I was at all.

I stood there for a minute; then I continued walking toward Trina's house to the party. It didn't make sense to me. The way Mama acted like she never met me or knew who I was. It was Mama that told me to get out of her sight and her house. That was why I left. I got over to Trina's house. A few of her other girl friends were there hanging out in the living room. I was the first dude to arrive, and I was glad when Trina started talking to me, even though I really didn't know what to say. Trina says; "Pee, can I talk to you about something?" "Yeah Trina, what is it?" I answered. Trina says; "What's the real deal with your family anyway? How come you're not at your house living with your parents?" I got upset after Trina said that to me. I just stayed quiet. Trina says; "You act like something is wrong all the time." "Trina, I'm ok." Then Trina says to me; "Pee, let's just get back to the party and have a good time."

I didn't want to tell Trina about all the crazy messed-up stuff that I was going through in my personal life. I felt too ashamed to tell anyone; that was why I didn't tell the people in the hospital when they asked. It hurt too much to even speak about the things I experienced in that house with Papa. People were able to see beyond the mask I was wearing. First Chad and now Trina were starting to ask me too many questions. It was making me feel uncomfortable being around them. I made up my mind a long time ago. I would not trust or get close to people after the way Mama and Papa treated me. The only person I trusted was Pee, Penny and only I.

Besides, I knew the day was approaching fast that I would have to move out of Chad's house to be on my own. I had been thinking about leaving Chad's place for a long time. Chad and I weren't getting along too well since I got out of the hospital. I was getting tired of all the questions about what happened to me in Mama and Papa's house.

I walked back to Chad's place after Trina's party was over. Trina and I had spent a lot of time joking and talking. I walked in the living room to sit down on the sofa. Chad was watching TV and never spoke one word to me. Then I decided to speak to him; "Hey Chad, what's up how are things going?" Chad says; "Pee, you know about me and Trina right?" I didn't know what Chad was talking about. "No, I don't know anything about you or Trina; you never told me." Chad yells; "Pee, why are you always acting like you're stupid? I know you know that Trina and I are going out." "Chad, that's cool. I just went to the party. Nothing happened. We were just talking."

I was glad indeed suddenly, that all we did was talk. Chad says "Nothing went down yet. How do I know you weren't thinking about going out with Trina, Pee?" I yelled; "Chad, what's wrong you? Why are you talking to me so stupid? I wouldn't betray you or Trina. I thought you both were my friends." Chad says; "You mean we used to be friends. Get your stuff, Pee. It is time you left."

It was almost the exact same words I remember Mama saying to me the day I left. "Chad, dude, you need to calm down. I have nowhere to go. Where am I supposed to live? On the streets?" Chad says; "That's your problem Pee, you should have thought of that before you started liking my girlfriend." "Chad, you know me better than that. I can't believe you are going to let some girl ruin our friendship. Chad, you never told me that Trina or you were in a serious relationship."

We both stood there quiet for a minute until Chad says; "The reason why I let you stay in my house was I felt sorry for you, dude. I knew about your Papa and the stuff that was happening in that crazy house. I just don't understand why you kept living with them Pee, after they treated you so bad." I yell "SHUT UP! Chad, this is not about my Mama or Papa, it's about Trina, you and me. You don't know all the hell those people put me through. I didn't know what I was supposed to do. I had no choice!"

Chad says; "Penny, I can't help you anymore it's starting to mess me up in my head. You're old enough to be on your own. I don't want anything else to do with you or your crazy life." "Chad, if this is the person you are and what you want, you're not the person I thought you were anyway. I never trusted you anyway. I will leave." Chad yells; "Pee, I want you out of my house before I come back home."

Chad then walked out the front door, leaving me standing there in shock about what the heck just happened. It was my own fault; how could I have been that stupid and not realize that Chad and Trina were in a relationship? I walked downstairs, gathered up my blanket and the few pieces of clothing I was given by Chad. Even the clothes I was wearing belonged to Chad. I quickly changed them. I put on the same clothes I had on the day I left my Mama and Papa's house. I wanted to be out of Chad's house before he came back home.

When I got back upstairs I looked around for a second. I walked out of Chad's front door, not knowing where I was going to be living next. There were lots of people hanging out at the park that were my age that night. I decided to go hangout in the park, too. When I got there, I walked over to a bench and sat down. I was trying to figure out where I was going to be living next. There was no way I was going back to the way I was living at that house. No way!

I lay down on the blanket I put on the bench. There was so much noise in the park that night; it kept me awake the entire night. The next day I woke up feeling hungry. I didn't know how I was going to get food. I had no money. I started walking through the park hoping I would see someone I knew. If I saw anyone I knew, I could ask them for money to buy food. Nobody I saw in the park was anybody I felt comfortable enough to ask for food on that day.

I decided then to go hangout in front of the grocery store. I stood there watching people going in and out of the store. I saw Mama walk into the store and I yelled; "Mama, wait a minute." Mama kept on walking into the store as if she never heard me. I was used to being ignored by people. Why should this time be any different? I just knew Mama would give me money to buy food when she came out of the grocery store. Mama walks out of the store I ran in front of her and asked "Mama it's me, Pee. I'm hungry can you give me some money for food?" Mama stares at me like I was crazy and then says; "Pee? I don't know nobody named Pee. I don't know who you are, move out of my way."

It hurt me when I heard Mama talk to me this way. I said; "Mama it's me. I'm your son, Penny. What are you talking about? I know that you know who I am, Mama." Mama looks right into my eyes with her eyes full and says; "Boy, I don't know who you are. I do not have a son named Pee. Get out of my way and leave me alone." I stepped out of Mama's way so she could walk on by. I just watched as Mama walked away with the bag of food in her hands. I just stared in shock watching Mama walk away. All I could think was I have seen and heard it all. Mama's words troubled me; "I do not have a son named Pee."

The hurt and anger I was feeling was as if someone had taken a knife and drove it through my heart. I wished there was a big rock that I could crawl under and never wake up again. I had no clue how I was going to survive or eat. I went back to the park bench and tried to go to sleep for the night. I walked over to the trash can at the park and found something in the trash on that night to eat. There was a bunch of older dudes smoking pot; getting high in the park. The smell of the pot woke me up it was so strong. I walked over to the guys getting high and ask if I could get high with them. As I got closer to where all the guys were standing, they all stopped talking and turned around and stared at me.

I asked; "Do you think I could get high with you guys?" This one dude named Tiny answered; "You're just a kid. You can't get high with us. Go back home. What are doing hanging out here anyway?" "I'm living in this park, Tiny. This is my new home." Tiny and his friends laughed, and then passed me the pot. We all got high together. My new life in the park consisted of begging for food, going to sleep hungry, not showering, sleeping on a park bench and getting drunk or high on pot.

Every day at the park I would try to find people that would get me high as often as possible. This went on for days and then days turned into weeks. I didn't even know what day or month it was anymore. I started to lose track of time and days. The person I had turned into was cold hearted. I did not care anymore. I felt absolutely nothing as I tried to survive from day to day. I turned eighteen years old living at the park; sleeping on that same bench.

The clothes I was wearing were starting to stink. They hadn't been washed in months. The smell of the dirty nasty rags I was wearing was making me sick to my stomach. I needed a bath or a shower. I couldn't stand to smell myself. I kept trying to hang out with the dude Tiny I met in the park. Tiny kept avoiding me and his friends laughed at me too. Nobody wanted me around them at the park. I would sit there on that bench waiting for somebody to walk by me with food hoping the person would throw the food in the trash or on the ground. If they did, I would wait until the person walks away, then run over and snatch the food up and eat it.

I started having flash backs about the basement and the day Papa beat me. I kept trying to dismiss the thought, but the words just kept racing in my mind over and over again. Papa said; "HUSH your mouth! Love is why I beat you," then I felt mad enough to destroy anything that got in my way. I swore to myself on that day; "Not Papa's or nobody else's love will ever beat me that way ever again or get away with it." How could someone beat you to the point of almost dying and then proclaim they beat you in the name of Love?

I knew in my mind at the moment what Love was and what Love was not. I also swore to myself on that day I would never love anyone after the way my Mama and Papa broke my heart. I hated Mama and Papa for not loving or caring for me the way I would always see other parents care for their children.

Chapter 5

Life in the Park

Nobody wanted to come near me in the park if they saw me. People would walk in the opposite direction. I couldn't blame them and I knew exactly why they would walk in the other direction. People knew I was going to asked them for food or money or to get high. It was obvious to me people did everything within their power to avoid running into me. I didn't have one person that I could depend on or trust in this world. Nobody would call me Pee, or Penny anymore. The new name people started calling me was Dirty P or skid row bum, Pee.

I was starting to lose touch with reality and society, fast. A day wouldn't go by without someone trying to attack me or making fun of me, including throwing things at me. I became used to them yelling; "Go take a bath, Dirty Pee." What those people didn't realize was I would have taken a bath if I had a place to take one. There was not one person that would have let me come over their house to take a shower. It was my eighteenth birthday and I was starving as I sat on the bench at the park. Hoping somebody would walk by me or throw some pocket change or food in my direction.

Then this couple walked by the bench where I was sitting. They both were eating a hamburger. I still remember how good it smelled on that day. Then I thought; Wow, it's been over a year since I ate a hamburger. The smell of it made me hungrier. There was a trash can not far from the bench were I was sitting. I watched as the couple walked over to the trash can. Then the guy throws away the rest of his hamburger and he walks away.

I looked around to see if anybody was looking at me. I ran over to the trash can and reached my hand into the trash can. I pulled out the hamburger the man threw away. I ran back to the bench; sat down and said out loud, Happy Birthday, Dirty P. I ate the rest of the hamburger the man threw in the trash on the day of my birthday. It didn't matter to me anymore, that man's trash had become my birthday dinner. I knew I was starting to lose my mind. The sad reality was nobody around me cared if I did.

Reality hit me hard on the day I turned eighteen. I accepted the fact I was a total bum eating out of trash cans. I had gotten so bad. I found myself living low as a person could ever go. At least, that was what I thought until I met this older man living on the streets. I got off my bench to go check if I could find some more food for the night. When I returned to my bench I saw an old man lying on the bench that I slept on every night for a year.

I started yelling at him; "Get off my bench, I always sleep there." The man just looked up at me and smiled, never said a word. It made me more upset. I said to the old man on the bench again, louder; "OFF MY BENCH." The man just looked at me, smiling. I asked the older man; "What is wrong with you? Are you deaf or something?" The older man pointed his hand toward his mouth then I realized the older man couldn't speak.

I felt like a total fool. I said to the older man; "Just stay there. I will sleep on the ground somewhere." I walked away from the older man resting on the bench I always slept on, thinking to myself what has happened to me that my life has ended up like this? When I got to the other side of the park, I was trying to find an empty bench. I saw these young kids just hanging out in the park. I wanted to walk by them fast then this one kid yells, loud; "Look, there goes Dirty Pee." They all started laughing at me. I stood still. All the kids ran over to me until they had me surrounded. I thought they were going to rob me. I said to them, I don't have any money, leave me alone. Then this kid that looked about sixteen years old says to me; "Dirty Pee, don't you want a drink of water, bum?" I answered no, I am not thirsty.

Life in the Park

The kids that surrounded me had water bottles in their hands, it was hot that night. Then the kid says; "Sure you do, Dirty Pee; let us give you some water." Then the kids all took their water bottles and aimed them toward me, throwing water on me from every direction. I just stood there until they were done. After they got finished throwing the water on me, they walked away laughing. This one kid as he passed me says; "Dirty Pee, now you had your bath for the night." I never felt so ashamed and humiliated in all my life.

Things just kept getting worst for me; it seemed there was never an end to my heartaches or misery. Those kids that threw the water on me didn't even realize I was just an eighteen year-old boy. I looked awful. Nobody would have believed that I was eighteen, anyway. The world saw me as dirty, good for nothing. Pee, the bum whom is always looking for food or money that sleeps on the bench at the park. I thought living on the streets was going to be easy. I found out the hard way I was so wrong. I ended up staying up the entire night thinking; what I'm going to do if that same bunch of kids comes back tonight to pick on me again at the park.

The next day came; I was thinking about that it had been almost a year since I have seen Papa, Mama, Chad or Trina. Chad came to hang out at the park that day. I couldn't believe it. I saw Chad, but he didn't even recognize me at all. I hesitated to go over to speak to Chad; I wasn't sure how he was going to react toward me. Then I thought, I'll walk over to Chad and try to talk with him. I said to Chad; "What's up? It's me Penny, how are you doing?"

Chad just stared at me like he didn't know who I was, or what I was talking about. Then Chad said; "Dude, I don't know who you are." "We grew up together, hung out parties, why don't you know who I am?" Then Chad said; "Penny, you don't even look the same anymore." "I know Chad. I've just been living here at the park for over a year. A lot of things have happened to me since then."

Then Chad said; "Your Father is in the hospital. He had a heart attack. They don't know if he is going to make it." "Chad, I don't care if Papa is in a hospital. He never cared about how he put me in the hospital." "I thought you knew about your father being in the hospital. Aren't you going to go see him?" "No Chad, I am never going to see Papa again." Chad said, "I have to leave. Do what you have to do. See you later."

After Chad walked away, I was thinking; why would anybody think I would go see Papa just because he is in the hospital? The only person I need to be worried or care about is me. Why did Papa treat me so bad? WHY? I just wanted to forget about what Chad said to me. I had to find a way to get high so I could forget. I ran into some dudes that were drinking beer. I got high with them until I passed out. I woke up the next day. I was in the hospital. I didn't have a clue where I was or what had happened the night before. The nurse came in and said to me, "Penny, you're finally awake. You're a very lucky young man to be living after all the drugs you took."

What are you talking about I said, then the nurse says; "We pumped your stomach last night. You took an overdose of Valium and almost died." "Who was it that found me and called the ambulance?" The nurse said; "It was an older gentleman he wouldn't give us his name. He also didn't speak. I think he is still sitting out in the waiting room. Do you want me to go tell him you're awake? I think he would like to come in and see if you're ok." I asked the nurse to tell him to come in. I want to speak to him and thank him for all he did for me. The nurse went to get the older gentlemen; he wasn't anywhere to be found in the waiting room. The nurse came back and said; "He was there a minute ago, now he is gone. I am not sure where he went. I'll be back to check in on how you are doing in a little while." I sat there in the room in the hospital thinking it had to be the older man I saw sleeping on the bench at the park.

They kept me in the hospital for a week. I was glad at least I had clean clothes and food. Then my day of discharge came. The doctor asked me; "Where will you be staying Penny?" I quickly made up a lie and said; "I will be going back to my parents' house." I knew I was going back to that same bench I lived on for a year. Chad or Trina never came to see me in the hospital. It didn't surprise me at all. Chad was acting angry toward me. I knew he was embarrassed to tell people he even knew me. Why would anyone waste their time coming to see me? I was only Dirty Pee that nobody loved or cared about anyway.

I got back to the park and went over to the bench I was used to living on. As I sat there, the old man I saw before sleeping on the bench walk by me. I hollered; "Hey wait a minute, I want to talk to you about something." The old man stops and waited until I rushed over to him. I got to where the old man was and asked him; "Did you call the ambulance when I took an overdose on that night I went to the hospital?"

The old man didn't answer me. I asked again; "Please tell me, was it you that called to get me help on that day?" The old man never answered. I thought as the old man walked away; he seems strange, it's probably best that I stay away from him. I needed to figure out where I was going to get something to eat for the night.

Chad and Trina came to the park. I saw them from a distance. I just didn't think that they would walk over to speak to me. Trina says; "How is everything going, Pee?" "Fine, Trina. I'm getting real used to being out here at the park." Trina said; "You are going to your Father's funeral, aren't you?" "Trina, what are you talking about; my Father's funeral?" "Your Father, he died of heart attack. Didn't you know?"

I stayed silent for a minute. I asked Trina if she knew where the funeral was going to be held. Trina said; "At the Gospel Way Church. That is where your Mother made arrangements for it to be." Chad, just kept staring at me and never spoke a word to me. Not even hello. "Trina, I doubt if I will be going to the funeral. I am sure Mama has everything planned nice for Papa." Trina says; "We have to go. Take care."

I said goodbye, and went looking for some drugs to get high. I was in troubled inside my heart. All I kept thinking about was Papa's funereal. I stayed high for five days. When I finally sobered up, it was the following week. Then I started to remember about the conversation Trina and I had at the park. Papa was dead. He never said sorry or anything to me about the way he treated me. I really didn't care that Papa was gone; at least now there will be nobody beating me in the name of Love. A tear came to my eye. I wasn't sure if it was a tear of joy or sorrow.

I was relieved that I didn't have to look over my shoulder. I worried everyday about a man I called Papa beating me in the name of Love. My heart just didn't feel right. I did not know how to think or feel anymore. I just sat on the bench wishing my name and life had been different and better.

Chapter 6

Love healed me

The old man walked over to me and sat beside me on the bench. I looked over at him and I saw he had a pencil and paper in his hand. The old man handed me the paper. I looked at the words he wrote. It said; "If I want happiness in my life I have to forgive those who have hurt me." I balled up the paper in my hand and threw it on the ground. I was mad and when I looked up, the old man was gone again.

I didn't understand who this old man was and why did he give me that note on that day. I never told him anything about my life or Mama or Papa. I walked over and picked the piece of paper off the ground and read the words again the old man wrote. "If I want happiness in my life I have to forgive those who have hurt me." I folded the paper and put it in my pocket. I'm not sure why I put the paper in my pocket.

The rest of day and night, those words that old man gave me in that note troubled me deep in my heart. I had a pencil and paper that the hospital had given to me on the day I was there. I decided to write a note to myself. I couldn't sleep. When I finished writing it surprised me as I read. These were the words I read on the paper on that day.

MISSING LOVE CHILD

I came into the world and didn't have a clue where I was going. I learned to walk, crawl and to speak. You claim you always Loved me; provided shelter and food to eat. I was a good boy and went to school every day. I brought home my school papers. You just tell me "HUSH YOUR MOUTH, JUST GO AWAY."

MISSING LOVE CHILD

As a boy, I just wanted to run, jump, and play like the other children. As I listened to their laughter from the basement every day, I told myself tomorrow will come and be a better day. A better day never came for me; I ended up living on the streets.

MISSING HUGS

I kept hoping and wishing Mama or Papa would hug me someday. You told me; "I'm busy right now, boy. Get out of my sight! HUSH YOUR MOUTH, GO AWAY!" What was I supposed to do? I turn and walk away.

MISSING TREATS

I went without food, because you wouldn't feed me. Many times, I would go to bed hungry. I tossed and cried my eyes to sleep. Then I hid the food for later that my stomach was too upset to eat. There were so many times you treated me bad or hurt and beat me.

MISSING PEACE

I thought it was normal in my mind. I believed in my heart beatings were the way Life was supposed to be. Today, I know my life is empty and I was determined to be free.

MISSING LOVE

I can't remember a time in my life as a child that I was HAPPY OR SMILED. I never believed that I was more special than any other child. I still tried to live each day knowing in my heart that soon this pain would be over. I was a **MISING LOVE CHILD**.

Author: Eugene McDuffie, 2006

When I finished reading what I wrote, it was like a bolt of lightning going through my heart and entire body. I looked at my surroundings at the park. I thought, I can't continue to live this way. I have to change my life or I am going to die in this park. The words the old man wrote to me stuck with me. It was all I kept thinking about.

How am I going to forgive those that have wronged me? Papa is gone now, and Mama wants nothing to do with me. Chad and Trina think I am lower than dirt; they do everything in their power to avoid me. Another day came and I was determined to do something to help myself. I just was not sure how to begin. I was rehearsing in my mind what I would say if I did run into Mama on the streets. I thought first I would try to talk with Chad without Trina being with him. It seems to me they were always together every time I saw them.

I was sitting on the bench at the park hoping Chad would walk through the park. Then eventually, he did. I ran over to him. I asked Chad; "Have you seen my Mama?" Chad said; "The last time that I saw her she didn't look very well." "What do you mean she doesn't look well?" Chad said; "The drugs and pills and alcohol your Mother has been taken are making her very sick." "Where is she at now? Do you know?" Chad said; "I don't know. I got to go. Bye."

I started thinking about how I hated the times I watched Mama drink liquor or pop those pills in her mouth. Then Mama would always change or talk to me mean or side with Papa. I really felt messed-up in the head like I was losing my mind. I hated that about myself the most. While I was lost in thought, the old man showed up. It seemed to me this guy was always showing up at certain times unexpected. I said to the old man; "What is your name anyway?"

The old man did not answer me and just walked over to sit down on the other side of the bench. I asked the old man again; "Hey, you never told me what your name is. What is your name?" Then some kids walked by the bench that me and the old man were sitting on and said; "You're crazy like that old crazy Lion man if you think he can talk, you are nuts, Pee." The kid and his friends laughed at us as they walked away. I told the old man on the bench not to pay any attention to those kids. They're just mean.

I never understood how a person's joy or laughter would come to them out of someone else's hurt or pain. I understood that maybe the reason this old man is not speaking or talking is because people are always embarrassing or laughing at him. I knew how the old man was feeling. I was never allowed to talk either. I was always saying the wrong thing at the wrong time. Maybe this old man was like me, a voice that just stopped talking because nobody was listening.

The old man looked into my eyes. I could feel in my heart and hear his silent words and scream. The old man stuttered as he spoke and said; "Lion, is my name, its Lion." I was shock for a second then Lion said; "Follow me, Pee." The old man jumped up quick off the bench. I followed him. I had not a clue where we were headed. We ended up in front of this soup kitchen. Lion, the old man, was taking me to a place where I could get food for the night.

I didn't even realize it as Lion and I walked into the building. Lion sat down at the table. I did too. This guy gets up in front of all of us waiting for the soup and says "Who will ask the blessing over the soup tonight?" I chuckled and commented to Lion that wouldn't be me.

The guy asked again; "We need someone to volunteer to say the Blessing over the soup." There were a lot of people waiting to get this soup; everybody was getting upset as we all waited. All of sudden this one guy yells out; "Lion, say the Prayer tonight." Lion was volunteered before either of us realized it, to say a prayer over the bowl of soup that night. I looked over at Lion and yelled out; "Get someone else to do it. Lion's not feeling well tonight. Get somebody else to do it."

There must have been over a hundred people in that building on that day. The people continued yelling out Lion's name. Some people even had the nerve to stand up cheering, yelling Lion's name. I thought to myself, we have to get out of this place. These people just want to make fun of Lion and me. I said Lion; "Let's leave, we will find something to eat somewhere else." Lion never said a word back to me. I looked at Lion like he was crazy as he stood his body up. Lion started walking toward the front of all those people. The people laughed as Lion walked by them and I could feel my entire body shaking.

All I could do was watch as the people continue to heckle and laugh. One person yells out; "Hurry up, crazy Lion. We want to eat this year." I knew Lion stuttered as he spoke, but those crazy people did not care if Lion did stutter. All they wanted to do was get that soup and nothing else mattered. I couldn't believe how brave Lion was as he walked up to the front of the room. I felt a tear come to the corner of my eye as I watched Lion put his head down to say the prayer. The nasty crowd of people started yelling and laughing at Lion. Then he stuttered these words loudly from a song I heard as a young boy.

I used to like to sing as a little boy, the words Lion stuttered; "For the bible tells me so," that was all Lion said. Suddenly it became very quiet in the room. I looked all around, nobody was laughing at Lion anymore. It was just so quiet. Nobody spoke one word as we ate that night in the soup kitchen. Back to the streets Lion and I headed after we finished eating the bowl of soup. The first person I saw back in the park was my friend Chad.

I should have known then something was wrong by the look on Chad's face. Chad never came to the park to see me anymore. Chad walked over to me and asked me; "Have you heard about your Mother, Pee?" I replied; "What are you talking about? What about my Mother?" Chad says; "Dude, they found your Mother passed out on the street and rushed her to the hospital." I wanted to say something back to Chad. Not one word would come out of my mouth. It was almost as if someone had cut my tongue off. I just could not speak a word no matter how hard I tried.

Chad starts yelling at me. "DID YOU HEAR ME? YOUR MOTHER IS IN THE HOSPITAL." I still did not respond to Chad. There were no words that could make my mouth speak. Then Chad walks away from me yelling; "You're CRAZY. I am through talking to you, Pee." I sat down on the bench to close my eyes and heard all the words Mama spoke to me in my head. "Pee, your Papa and I decided you are going to have to sleep downstairs in the basement. Because our family is going to be staying here in the house we need this room…"

Chapter 7

Missing Light in My Life

I continued to think about what Mama said; "Pee, go show my nephew the room he is going to be sleeping in while he is staying with us. You know; the room that I fixed up for him. ANSWER ME, ARE YOU DEAF, PEE, OR JUST STUPID. You could never be a good boy! Pee, you disgust me. Your Papa or I NEVER WANTED a boy. GET OUT OF MY HOUSE, BEFORE I HURT YOU. I have no son named Pee."

The thoughts kept racing through my mind over and over again. I just couldn't get Mama's nasty, hateful words to me out of my head. I sat up on the bench opened my eyes and then spoke these words out loud to myself. My words were; NO WAY! I am not going to that hospital. Days have gone by. Often I would think about Mama in the hospital. I dismiss the thoughts quickly. I was not going to see her in the hospital, after the way Mama treated me and let Papa do all the awful things to me. I hated Mama and Papa just as much as they hated me.

I went over to the trash can to look for some food to eat. I found a bagel someone threw in the trash. Then I thought, WOW! This is bad. Someone's dirty bagel, I just picked out of the garbage has now become my main meal for the day. Damn, my life was so messed up just like the garbage in the trashcan. I spent weeks with my mind in a fog. All reality was gone. Often I could not even remember how I got through the day or if I ate or not.

Trina, Chad's girlfriend comes walking toward me at the park. I was hoping Trina would just go by me. Instead Trina yells; "PEE, I have to tell you something." I asked Trina; "What you are talking about? Tell me what?" Trina says; "Your Mother." I interrupted Trina and said; "I do not want to hear anything about my Mama. I have no Mother or Father; it is only just me and only me!"

Then Trina just stares out at me and says; "Pee, you are right. It is only just you. Your Mama died in the hospital last night of a heart attack." Then Trina walked away from me and never turned around to look back at me.

My entire body began to shake like crazy. My knees felt like they were not a part of my body anymore. I could no longer stand. I sat down on the bench at the park. My heart was beating so fast and loud all I could hear was my heartbeat. I didn't know what to think or do anymore. I sat on the bench for days. My mind kept thinking about that crazy house, the basement, and Papa. I lost track of the time I did not sleep for days. Until Chad tapped me on the shoulder and says; "Pee, snap out of it. Today is your Mother's funeral. Are you going?"

"Chad, I'm not going to Mama's Funeral. I have other things to do." Then Chad just stares at me angrily and turns around and leaves. I just kept thinking about Mama as I sat on the bench. I just wanted to walk to try to clear my mind. I started walking anywhere. I did not care where I was going because I had no place to go. I just wanted to walk because I thought the walk would make me tired. It always baffles me how we could be thinking we are walking in one direction with our feet. Yet our mind walks us in another direction.

I think the reason that happens to us is because our feet don't really do all the walking like we think. The fact of the matter is our mind tells our feet where to go. This was the place I ending up walking to. In my heart, I didn't want to walk the path I was going. Then there I stood in front of the funeral home that my Mama was lying in a coffin in. I tried to turn around and leave, but my feet would not move. I just stood at those big, double doors.

I spoke out loud to myself; "Just go in that funeral home and see your Mama." I felt a wind push me inside those double doors and then from a distance, I could see Mama in the coffin. There were other people sitting inside the funeral home that came to say goodbye to Mama. I didn't know any of the people in the funeral home. As I was standing there at the funeral home I watched people turn around and whisper to each other. I already knew they were whispering about me. I heard one lady say; "I can't believe her son Pee came to his Mama's funeral looking like that." I wanted to run out of the funeral home.

Then people started leaving the funeral home and I was still standing in that same spot. I looked around the room and everyone was gone. It was just Mama lying in the coffin and me standing in the same spot. I started walking toward the coffin Mama was lying in. The closer I go to the coffin, the madder I got. I stood there in front of Mama and stared at her in the coffin. The tears ran down my cheeks and fell on my Mama's face. I couldn't believe I was crying.

These are the words I said to Mama on that day of her passing away. I said; "Mama, for every time you did not hug me or tell me you loved me. Sometimes you would never even say goodnight. I slept down in that cold, dirty basement. Papa would come downstairs to laugh at me. I know you must have known the reason why he was always buckling up his pants.

The bad way Papa was touching me that make me urinate on myself. Mama, for the time you threw me out of your and Papa house. I remember the day I was so hungry and I saw you Mama, shopping at the store. You told me on that day that you did not have a son named Penny.

Mama, I forgive you! Mama, you knew Papa was the one that beat me up. Mama, why do you choose to stay quiet and not protect me? I was your son. WHY? Mama, I forgive you! Mama, on this day these will be the last words that I will ever speak to you. I remember Mama, your big family reunion was more important than me, your only son. The day I came home with my art project from school that broke. My heart broke on that night into a thousand pieces. I was nobody's child.

Nobody cared about what happened to me. Mama, you put your relatives in my bed to sleep. Mama, for every hurt and everything you spoke or Papa did to me...Mama, in my heart I choose to forgive you and Papa!"

I started walking away from Mama and I never looked back. I was walking to the bench at the park to go to sleep. My body felt as light as a feather! I was thinking about ways I could get myself cleaned up. Maybe I could get a job or a place to live; I just was not sure how to go about it. I finally felt maybe now I could find peace and happiness for my life. I just did not know how to think or feel. I felt totally strange.

I was so used to being bitter; it felt strange not to have all the hateful thoughts going through my mind. Finally, I went back to the park, and sat down on the bench. I was hoping Lion would be there, but he was not. My mind and body felt exhausted.

As I was sitting on the bench at the park; I saw this bright flash of light in front of my face. I closed my eyes then I tried to open my eyes, but the light was too bright. It blinded me. I could not open my eyes. I could hear my heart speeding up. I was scared. I did not know what was happening to me. I opened my eyes, and then the same bright, shining light appeared to me again.

This time I saw such beautiful colors like the human eye has never seen. Amazing colors I saw that made me feel hope and love and peace. I saw colors that no hand had ever painted on any picture. Then I heard these words spoken to me from the bright, beautiful, marvelous light. The words spoken to me from the bright, shining, marvelous, light were:

"Penny, for every time you lied and hurt others. Penny, my child; I forgive you! Penny, for the hate, hurt, and bitterness you carried in your heart, Penny, my child; I forgive you! Penny, for the way you denied me and rejected my love, Penny my child; I forgive you!"

I started remembering the story I would sometimes hear as a young child. The story about how there was someone higher than me and who loved the entire world. *He gave his only begotten Son, that whosoever believeth in him should not perish, but have everlasting life.* Then I heard the voice speak to me again; "Penny my child; Accept my Love, Penny! My Love can heal your mind and broken heart." Then that same light covered my entire body. I could feel the heat from the light going through my blood and veins. I opened my eyes and felt like a newborn baby.

I did not understand everything that happened to me on that day as I sat on the bench. I just knew in my heart and mind that I would never be the same again. Or think the same, or live the way I was living anymore. I got up and stared for a second at that bench I called my home. I looked all around at the park. Everything looked so different to me. I spoke these words out loud to myself; "I am going to learn to walk and live in the light of that Love that burned in my heart though a bright shining light. A broken piece of clay can be used and shaped all over again into something beautiful. It has been many years; I am no longer a scared young boy. I know now the unconditional love. The power of that light can heal any hurt or pain you or I may ever face in our lives on this world. I know the light of that love is so miraculous that it can heal a boy like me. Even a boy named Penny. A pure unconditional life changing love I embrace from Heaven above."

I have learned that infants become extremely attached to those who respond in an appropriate manner to their behaviors and current needs. The bond that a child has with its caregiver will impact the child for the rest of their life. Children develop an attachment to those they respond to people who show them attention and respond to their individual needs. The way that a mother or father interacts with her child is a factor.

I have also learned that children who have a secure attachment to both parents will develop higher self-esteem. The process begins for children in infancy. An infant may understand something by its prior knowledge that it had already at birth, like how an infant knows the voice and face of its mother. In secure attachment, the child feels safe if its mother is around and upset if she is not. This is where my story begins. Penny's words to me were in the beginning of his story; "I never had love, Mr. Eugene; **"Love was MISSING in my life."** As Penny continued to speak to me he said; "The Bright Light of love is Jesus! The Miraculous Light of Love is Jesus; it healed a boy like me named Penny." I know Penny is like so many other children. Some have grown up and become adults, or maybe some are still children. Any Adult or Child can experience the light of that Miraculous Healing Love. A Healing Power that can change and heal a broken heart and life forever.

I believe there may be people today who may be able to relate to Penny's story. I hope someday you too; will find the Miraculous light of healing love in your life. Over the years, one truth among many I have learned; there is a very special bond that takes place between an infant and its caregiver that helps with a child's cognitive, emotional, social development. You no longer need to "Hush your mouth," the way Penny was always told to do! If you're living a life like that; people are hurting you.

Do not keep silent! Seek out the Authorities or Professional medical help. After all, you deserve and have a right to speak out if anyone is harming you. Remember, the greatest gift you can give any child is a gift of Love. There is no reason in this world that anyone needs to hush their mouth!

Author: Eugene McDuffie 2001-2007/2013

www.ingramcontent.com/pod-product-compliance
Ingram Content Group UK Ltd.
Pitfield, Milton Keynes, MK11 3LW, UK
UKHW041956230426
12048UKWH00008B/365